In the Day of

Thy Power

Ministries
From
Psalm 110

LANCE LAMBERT

ISBN 978-0-9889290-5-0

Available from:

Christian Testimony Ministry
4424 Huguenot Road
Richmond, Virginia 23235

www.christiantestimonyministry.com

Printed in USA

Contents

INTRODUCTION

This book grew out of a series of studies given on Psalm 110, at Halford House, Richmond, Surrey, England, some fifty years ago, and repeated in the Christian Family Conference, in Richmond, Virginia, USA, and elsewhere. I have sought to turn it into a more readable form.

There is no matter as practically important as this subject. The enthroned Lamb is to be found everywhere in the last book of the Bible, which sums up everything from Genesis to Jude. It is not only however the theme of the book of Revelation; the seated and triumphant Messiah Jesus underlies the whole of the New Testament, from the Gospels until the book of Revelation. The dogmatic proclamation that Jesus is Lord, that He is seated and has won, is found everywhere in the New Testament. The Old Testament likewise, in all its thirty-nine books, is focused on the Messiah and His coming. All is summed up in the words of John the Baptist: "Behold, the Lamb of God, that taketh away the sin of the world!" (John 1:29). This fascinating little Psalm, Psalm 110, gathers up all this in its seven verses. It is both prophetic and Messianic. Is it any wonder that it is the most quoted Psalm in the New Testament?

The sad fact is that most Christian believers have little understanding and experience of the enthroned Messiah Jesus and His triumph. For many it is a doctrine, true but distant. The problem is whether to leave it as a doctrine, without practical expression or realization; or whether by living faith to be in practical union with the Lord Jesus and to know fully the glorious and powerful results of His finished work, His resurrection, and His ascension to the right hand of God. The early church clearly lived in the good and experience of His enthronement. Furthermore, in every great move of the Holy Spirit in the history of the church, the same reality has been known with tremendous consequences. Society has been turned upside down; nations have been impacted; the church has functioned truly as the body of the Lord Jesus; and believers have entered into the fullness and power of His life.

In the course of writing this book, for the sake of clarity, I have indulged in a certain amount of repetition. It seems to me that it is unavoidable if the true consequences of His enthronement and triumph are to be understood. My concern has been for the truth of Christ's present position at God's right hand, and the practical implications of it to be seen and experienced. There is no doubt that the lives of those first believers in the New Testament era were revolutionized by the seeing and realization of this truth; and so it has been throughout the history of the true and living church. May it be so with us!

I wish to acknowledge those who have helped in the final production of this book: Nathan Gosling of the UK who typed the manuscript and Joshua Fiddy of the UK, who looked after the house and garden in Naxos, whilst the work was being done; whilst Richard Briggs, of the UK and Shlomo Levine of the USA, looked after the home in Jerusalem.

May the Lord use this book to bring clearer understanding of His total triumph, and how we can appropriate all the fruit of His enthronement.

Lance Lambert
Jerusalem 2010

Chapter 1

JESUS THE ENTHRONED MESSIAH

Psalm 110:1-7–The Lord saith unto my Lord, Sit thou at my right hand,
Until I make thine enemies thy footstool.
The Lord will send forth the rod of thy strength out of Zion:
Rule thou in the midst of thine enemies.
Thy people offer themselves willingly
In the day of thy power, in the beauty of holiness;
Out of the womb of the morning
Thou hast the dew of thy youth;
The Lord hath sworn, and will not repent;
Thou art a priest for ever
After the order of Melchizedek.
The Lord at thy right hand
Will strike through kings in the day of his wrath.
He will judge among the nations,
He will fill the places with dead bodies;
He will strike through the head in many countries,
He will drink of the brook in the way;
Therefore will he lift up the head.

A word of prayer:

Father, as we come to Thy word and to this particular portion of Thy word, we want to confess, dear Lord, our absolute dependence upon the ministry of Thy Holy Spirit. We thank Thee, beloved Lord, that whether speaking or hearing Thou hast made a provision for us in the anointing which is ours in our Head, the Lord Jesus. And Father, by faith every one of us, young and old, would all stand together, speaker and hearer alike, into that anointing that we might know a portion of it, every one of us. We ask Thee, Lord, Thou would take Thy word and make it live to us. Cause Thy word to dwell in us, may it be a word that creates something within us. Oh Father, human words cannot do that but Thy word can. And therefore, Lord, we commit ourselves very simply to Thee in the name of our Lord Jesus. Amen.

A MESSIANIC PSALM

Psalm 110 is one of the most important Messianic Psalms found within the Psalter. That it refers to the Lord Jesus the Messiah is amply evidenced many times in the New Testament. If there is a question as to whether some of the other Messianic Psalms are truly Messianic, over this psalm there can be little doubt.

For example we read in Matthew 22:41-46 the words of our Lord Jesus Himself: "Now while the Pharisees were gathered together, Jesus asked them a question, saying, 'What think ye of the Messiah? whose son is he?' They say unto him, The son of David. He saith unto them, How then doth David in the Spirit call him Lord, saying,

The Lord said unto my Lord,
Sit thou on my right hand,
Till I put thine enemies underneath thy feet?

If David then calleth him Lord, how is he his son? And no one was able to answer him a word, neither durst any man from that day forth ask him any more questions."

The Lord Jesus states that this Psalm refers to the Messiah, and goes further than some of our modern Bible scholars, in saying that David is its author and that he was in the Spirit when he wrote it.

In the highly significant and powerful message that Peter preached on the day of Pentecost under the anointing of the Holy Spirit, he declares: "This Jesus did God raise up, whereof we all are witnesses. Being therefore by the right hand of God exalted, and having received of the Father the promise of the Holy Spirit, he hath poured forth this, which ye see and hear. For David ascended not into the heavens: but he saith himself,

'The Lord said unto my Lord,

Sit thou on my right hand,

Till I make thine enemies the footstool of thy feet.'

Let all the house of Israel therefore know assuredly, that God hath made him both Lord and Messiah, this Jesus whom ye crucified" (Acts 2: 32-36).

Again in the letter to the Hebrews, the writer says by the Spirit of God: "But of which of the angels hath he (that is God the Father) said at any time,

Sit thou on my right hand,

Till I make thine enemies the footstool of thy feet?" (Hebrews 1:13)

Then again, we have three more references in the Hebrew letter quoting this Psalm: "As he saith also in another place, Thou art a priest for ever after the order of Melchizedek" (Hebrews 5:6); and again in Hebrews 7:17 it declares: "For it is witnessed of him (that is Jesus), Thou art a priest for ever after the order of

Melchizedek." And again in verse 21: ("For they indeed became priests without an oath, but He with an oath through the One who said to Him, 'The Lord has sworn and will not change His mind, Thou art a priest forever" NASB).

We have therefore incontrovertible evidence in the New Testament that Psalm 110 is indeed a Messianic Psalm and that it refers to the Lord Jesus as the Messianic King, as great David's greater son; that it was spoken in the Spirit, and reveals His present position and power. This has vast meaning and significance for the Church and the true believer in this present age. If we believe in the full authority, inspiration and relevance of the Bible, this should be enough.

We can conclude therefore that Psalm 110 reveals and expresses the most tremendous and essential truth concerning Christ and His own.

RAISED UP AND MADE US TO SIT WITH CHRIST

It is not only that we have these references to Psalm 110 in the New Testament; the fact of the enthronement of the Lord Jesus at God's right hand is repeatedly emphasized throughout its twenty-seven books and letters and underlies the whole. Furthermore His enthronement is vitally and essentially related to the Church and the believer. It is not mere factual and impersonal truth and doctrine which transforms the life of a fellowship of God's people and the life of individual believers; it is the illumination and making real of that truth by the Holy Spirit, which transforms us. Practically linked to the enthroned and seated Messiah we overcome. Through the centuries, in the history of the true and living Church, there have been many incredible and glorious examples of this.

The Apostle Paul by the Holy Spirit declares that: "When he raised him from the dead, and made him to sit at his right hand in the heavenly places, far above all rule, and authority, and power, and dominion, and every name that is named, not only in this world, but also in that which is to come: and he put all things in subjection under his feet, and gave him to be head over all things to the Church, which is his body, the fullness of him that filleth all in all" (Ephesians 1:20-23).

Note that the enthronement of the Lord Jesus is related to the Church in its practical testimony, its life and its walk. Or again the Apostle Paul further states: "And raised us up with him, and made us to sit with him in the heavenly places in Christ Jesus" (Ephesians 2:6). It is important to note that he is not speaking of something in the eternal future, but of our practical experience now "in a world that lies in the Evil One."

<h3 align="center">THE LAMB ENTHRONED, THE KEY TO ALL</h3>

In the last book of the Bible, it is stated: "And one of the elders saith unto me, Weep not; behold the Lion that is of the tribe of Judah, the Root of David, hath overcome to open the book and the seven seals thereof. And I saw in the midst of the throne and of the four living creatures, and in the midst of the elders a Lamb standing, as though it had been slain ..." (Revelation 5:5-6).

It is a stunning fact that before we come to all the

turmoil, strife and conflict described in this book, in one sense horrifying, we see enthroned with God the Father, the little Lamb, the Lion of the tribe of Judah, who is Jesus the Messiah. The overcomers that we see throughout this book are the direct consequence of that enthronement. "And they overcame him because of the blood of the Lamb, and because of the word of their testimony; and they loved not their life even unto death" (Revelation 12:11).

The enthronement of the Lord Jesus at the right hand of God is the key to everything; whether it is the life of the Church on earth, or the life of individual believers, or the work of the servants of God. It is also the guarantee of the coming down from heaven of the New Jerusalem, the Bride of Christ, and the Wife of the Lamb. There is no way in which Satan and his hosts can thwart or frustrate the purpose of God. The Lamb has won, and within that victory is all we need to overcome, and see His purpose fulfilled.

THE PRACTICAL SIGNIFICANCE OF THE ENTHRONEMENT FOR US

Between the first two verses and the last two verses we find the announcement: "In the Day of His Power thy people are freewill offerings." In what manner are these people, who are described as volunteers, as freewill offerings, connected to the statement: "The Lord said to my Lord sit thou at my right hand until I make thine enemies thy footstool. The Lord will send forth the rod of thy strength out of Zion: Rule thou in the midst of thine enemies."

Furthermore the next verses proceed to speak of

the Messiah as both King and Priest. It is clear that the ascension and glorification of Jesus was the beginning of the "Day of His Power." In what way are His people involved? And why is it not all of the redeemed but only those who are prepared to be volunteers, to be freewill offerings? It is this connection and relationship which needs to be understood. How far are we to go? Are we meant to take governments and nations, to master and Christianize world society, its political, its social and its educational systems? Or are we meant to do nothing but wait for the return of the Messiah? Both extremes are dangerous!

It is of paramount importance that we come into a balanced understanding of the enthronement of the Lord Jesus, and its practical significance for us who live today in this fallen world. Is the triumph of the seated Messiah only to do with personal salvation, or has it tremendous and practical bearing on the many problems and difficulties which confront the work of God on this earth?

THE ABSOLUTE VICTORY OF THE ENTHRONED LAMB

Psalm 110 breathes the absolute victory of the enthroned Lamb. Within His triumph, and the simple fact that the Father says to Him: "Sit thou at my right hand until I make thine enemies thy footstool," everything we need for salvation, for deliverance, for healing, for transformation and for overcoming is found; all that we need for the work of the Gospel to advance, for the mountains of difficulty, whether international, national, or local to be removed, is within the reality of the Messiah's enthronement. It is the same with the planting and building of the Church. The end has been secured at the very beginning. We who are redeemed by God, who have been saved by the grace of God through the finished work of the Lamb, are not fighting a battle that is in question. Even though, at times, it seems as if Satan and his host have complete sway, and the whole world is swamped with evil, the end has been completely and absolutely secured right at the start. The guarantee of this is that our Lord Jesus Christ has sat down at the right hand of God the Father. The enthronement of the Lamb is an essential and fundamental fact. It is not something which we are imagining; something we proclaim as an ideal, with no practical effect; it is an unchanging, and unchangeable fact. It lies at the heart of the whole amazing progress and growth of the early Church, and of every move of the Holy Spirit in Church history ever since. Jesus has sat down at the right hand of God the Father. It is the discovery of this fact through the Holy Spirit which has birthed movements of revival and renewal again and again in the history of the Church.

THE LORD SEATED AT GOD'S RIGHT HAND

Carefully note the word sit. The Lord Jesus is not fighting, or struggling, or in nervous tension as to whether those whom He has saved will be able to reach the goal, and thus not frustrate His purpose. We only have one instance of His standing, and that was when He stood to receive Stephen the martyr. He may stand to intercede for us, but in the Word of God that is not made clear. The fact that the Father says: "Sit thou at my right hand until I make thine enemies thy footstool," proclaims the reality that Jesus has won the battle.

Wherever we turn in the New Testament we find this incredible and foundational truth. Mark concludes his Gospel with the statement: "So then the Lord Jesus, after he had spoken unto them, was received up into heaven, and sat down at the right hand of God. And they went forth, and preached everywhere the Lord working with them, and confirming the word by the signs that followed" (Mark 16:19). Note that the enthronement of the Lord Jesus, and the understanding by the disciples of that fact, resulted in their preaching, with the Word being confirmed by the signs that followed.

Again the Apostle Peter in his first letter states: "Through the resurrection of Jesus Christ; who is on the right hand of God, having gone into heaven; angels and authorities and powers being made subject unto him" (1 Peter 3:21b-22).

Or again, the Apostle Paul declares: "Then cometh the end, when he shall deliver up the kingdom to God even the Father; when he shall have abolished all rule and all authority and power. For he must reign till he hath put all his enemies under his feet. The last enemy that shall be abolished is death" (1 Corinthians 15:24-26).

The writer of the Hebrew letter also proclaims the fact: "But he (Jesus) when he had offered one sacrifice for sins forever, sat down on the right hand of God; henceforth expecting till his enemies be made the footstool of his feet. For by one offering he hath perfected forever them that are sanctified" (Hebrews 10:12-14).

The glorious truth that so thrilled and inspired the writers of the New Testament is the enthronement of the Lord Jesus at the right hand of God the Father. For them it was a most practical and powerfully influential truth. It affected their whole life corporately and personally. The Lord Jesus had finished the work, had won the battle, and had sat down. It was a perfect picture of complete relaxation and rest. The Enemy and the enemies could never dethrone the Lord Jesus or paralyze His work; Satan and his host could only touch the members of Christ's body on earth. Those believers would have to learn to live in the good of the enthronement of the Lamb. Everything they could ever need would be provided in that finished work, and in the power of the Holy Spirit. However it should be stated clearly that whatever the Lord Jesus has won, those who are born of God must possess; otherwise it will remain impersonal doctrine and academic truth with little practical effect. They would have to learn how to proclaim simply and powerfully that Jesus is Lord, that He has won, and is seated at God's right hand. The very proclamation of the fact will insure their spiritual safety, their security, and their victory.

THY FOOTSTOOL

God the Father says to the Son that He is to sit until He makes His enemies His footstool. It is a striking phrase "the footstool for your feet," literally "a stool for your feet." In the East, especially amongst oriental Jews and Arabs, to show the soles of your feet in a deliberate gesture is a serious offence; the most serious insult you can make. The Scriptures make mention of this many times, for example: "And whoever does not receive you, nor heed your words, as you go out of that house or that city, shake off the dust of your feet" (Matthew 10:14 NASB). In other instances, it speaks of His feet being placed upon the enemies of the Lord; Joshua told his generals to put their feet upon their enemies' necks. We have in the last few years seen shoes thrown by an angry Arab at even the president of the United States.

When God says that he will make the enemies of the Lord Jesus the stool for His feet, it means that they are absolutely defeated; they are shattered, and their power broken. The Father is saying to the Son You have won; Your work is so complete, so absolutely perfect, so comprehensive, that You are to sit at My right hand until, through that work, I make all Your enemies your footstool. We should note carefully that it is the Father who is doing this awesome work. One after another the enemies of the Lord Jesus are to be made the footstool of His feet. All through the history of the last two millennia, God has been taking the enemies of the Lord Jesus and making them His footstool. Whether, for instance, it was Nero, or Bloody Queen Mary, or Napoleon, or Adolf Hitler, or Joseph Stalin, or Lenin, or Mao Zedong, or Yasser Arafat, they have all come and they have all gone. There are many other enemies of Christ that we could mention; but the fact is simple, that in the end they all become the footstool of the Lord

Jesus.

THE LAMB HAS WON

When you come to the last book of the Bible, the book of Revelation, in the midst of all the turmoil, the conflict, the battle, and the martyrdom there is a marvelous statement. This statement expresses exactly the fact that Jesus has won the battle, and no matter how much the powers of darkness rage His purpose will be fulfilled.

"The voice of the seventh angel when he is about to sound, 'then is finished the mystery of God, according to the good tidings that were declared to his servants the prophets" (Revelation 10:7).

The Apostle John was in a forced labor camp being worked to death. He was in circumstances that were not the least bit conducive to spirituality, or to seeing genuine visions of God, or to understanding the purpose of God. It was there that God opened the heavens and John saw vision after vision, of which the most glorious of all was the throne of God, and in the midst of that throne a little Lamb as it had been slain, and the whole universe worshipping that Lamb. That little Lamb as slain, the Lion of Judah, is none other than the enthroned Messiah. The war, the rebellion against God, the violence, the turmoil and the conflict, was unable to stop the fulfillment of the purpose of God. He saw in the end the New Jerusalem coming down out of heaven having the glory of God. Every thing he saw was because the Lamb, the Lion of Judah, had won. It was as if God was saying: "Do not fear, John, even if they take the life of many faithful believers, the end is secure. Do not fear! You shall yet see Him on the throne saying: 'Behold I make all things new.' The Lamb has won!"

There is not one single digit to be added to the finished work of the Lord Jesus. It is complete and perfect. There is not a "t" to be crossed, or an "i" to be dotted. Every single thing that is necessary to save a depraved and bound sinner, has been accomplished; everything essential to turn a sinner into a saint has been completed; everything required to conform you and me to the image of God's Son has already been won by the blood of the Lamb. It is done! Everything required for the building and completion of the Church has been obtained. You cannot add a single letter to God's alphabet; Jesus is both the Alpha and the Omega! It is all completed: in that finished work of the Lord Jesus lies all your salvation, all your sanctification, all your anointing; and all that is required for the building up and completion of the Church.

I remember years ago that, one of our brothers who had been a womaniser, a drug addict, a gambler, and an alcoholic, had been gloriously saved and delivered. He became a very original brother, and every now and again around the Lord's Table he would contribute with the most extraordinary word of exhortation or comment. One day he spoke and said, "I was depressed and went out for a walk in the rain and mist, which did not help me. When I came back to my house, I heard laughter and excitement coming from inside. I went into the living room where the children were watching sports on television. They were showing the big national horserace, and I became quite excited as I watched the finish because the whole place was in an uproar. Two horses, side by side, went over the finish line, but they could not tell which one had won. It was a photo finish. They had to wait for the Judges decision. Then the verdict came: 'Such and such a horse has won by a nose.' This became such an enormous lesson to me; for the Lord said to me, 'When the head has gone over the finish line, the rest of the body has won, even the last hairs of the tail.' No matter how small or insignificant we are, if the Head has won, so have we!"

Now that is exactly what happened with the Lord Jesus. The Head, the Lord Jesus, has gone over the line and the rest of the body has won. Praise the Lord! We are in the good of the Head. He is invincible. Satan cannot touch the Head but he can touch us; he cannot hinder the Head but he can hinder us; he cannot frustrate the purpose of God for Jesus Christ, but he can meddle with us. We have to learn how to stand in the good of the finished work of Christ. We have to learn how to proclaim this simple but undeniable fact; Jesus has won, and is enthroned at the right hand of God.

THE CONSEQUENCES OF THE ENTHRONEMENT OF THE LORD JESUS

What are the consequences of our Lord Jesus sitting down at God's right hand? The results have enormous significance for all who are born of God.

WITH THE ENTHRONED CHRIST NOTHING IS IMPOSSIBLE

The first consequence underlies everything. The enthroned Lamb is invincible! There is nothing that He cannot do; no advance He cannot make, no obstacle He cannot overcome, no problem He cannot solve, no difficulty he cannot unravel and no mountain He cannot move. There is no principality or power that is not subject to Him and to His Name, which is above every name that can be named. The ascended, glorified and seated Messiah represents a total triumph over all the powers of darkness and evil. His sovereign authority extends over all His enemies, and there is nowhere the rod of His strength cannot reach. He has within His hands all the keys; the Key of David and even the Keys of Death and Hades.

Before the Lord Jesus ascended to the right hand of God and sat down at His right hand, He had already declared that: "All authority hath been given unto me in heaven and on earth" (Matthew 28:18). It is important to carefully note that His authority extends over a fallen earth which lies in the Evil One. He went on to command: "Go therefore and make disciples of all the nations,...and lo, I am with you always, even to the end of the age" (Matthew 28:19-20 NASB). It is of tremendous consequence that the enthroned Messiah, the Lord Jesus, promises to be with those who obey His command, whatever the cost may be, and follow Him. The Messiah seated at the right hand of God promises that all His power and authority is with them, even to the consummation of the age. That is no small promise! What He commands, for that He always provides. With the enthroned Christ nothing is impossible!

THE PROMISE OF THE FATHER OBTAINED AND POURED OUT UPON US

A second and glorious consequence of the Lord Jesus being enthroned at God's right hand is the pouring out of the Holy Spirit. Everything practical is connected with the person and the work of the Holy Spirit. The Lord Jesus is at the right hand of the Father, as the ascended and glorified Second Man. It is the Holy Spirit who makes everything about the Lord Jesus real to us and in us. Without the Holy Spirit there is nothing but religion. All through the Old Testament, the coming of the Holy Spirit upon people for certain purposes and tasks was experienced. It was the permanent and continual indwelling of the Holy Spirit in the believer that was not experienced. On the day of Pentecost two glorious matters were realized at one and the same time. The Holy Spirit came to permanently indwell saved human beings, and He came also to anoint and empower them to serve. It was a stunning and awesome consequence of the Lord Jesus being enthroned. The Apostle Peter on that actual day said: "Being therefore by the right hand of God exalted, and having received of the Father the promise of the Holy Spirit, He hath poured forth this, which ye see and hear..." He then goes on to quote Psalm 110 (see Acts 2:33-36).

During another of the festivals in the Temple, the festival of Succot, for seven days the Levites brought in great pitchers full of water and poured them out on the steps of the court of the women. On the last and eighth day, they came with their pitchers empty and went through the movement of pouring out the water, but there was no water. It represented the fact that the promise of the Father to pour out the Holy Spirit on all flesh had not yet been fulfilled. This ritual symbolised the promise of the latter rain, when the Holy Spirit would be poured out upon all, according to the prophet Joel. It was on that day, when the Levites poured out their empty pitchers, the great day of the feast that Jesus stood up and said: "If any man thirst let him come unto me and drink. He that believeth on me, from within him shall flow out rivers of living water. This spake He of the spirit, which had not yet been given, because Jesus had not yet been glorified" (see John 7:37-39). Note carefully that Jesus speaks not only of quenching our thirst, but of rivers of living water flowing out from within. It is not only that we are satisfied but there is something for others. The Apostle John's words should be heeded, "this spake He of the Spirit."

It is very hard to understand how Christians can be afraid of the Holy Spirit. His ministry and work is essential in the life of the Church, the work of God, and of the believer. The Lord Jesus Himself said: "Howbeit when He, the Spirit of truth, is come, He shall guide you into all the truth: for he shall not speak from himself; but what things soever He shall hear, these shall He speak: and He shall declare unto you the things that are to come. He shall glorify Me: For He shall take of Mine, and shall declare it unto you. All things whatsoever the Father hath are Mine: therefore said I, that He taketh of Mine, and shall declare it unto you" (John 16:13-15).

There are of course extremes, excesses, and counterfeits, at times associated with the subject of the work of the Holy Spirit. We have to learn how to discern and to distinguish between what is of the Spirit of God and what is not. Nevertheless to decide to ignore the work of the Holy Spirit, or even to reject His work, is spiritual suicide. It means that we cut ourselves off from the one and only ministry that keeps us abiding in Christ, and alive in Him. We do not stop eating because food poisoning is one of the most common killers; we learn to eat well and wisely, and live as a result!

THE GIFTS AND EQUIPMENT OF THE HOLY SPIRIT

Within the poured out Holy Spirit all the gifts and equipment we need for the ministry of Christ and for His service, are provided. It is already given to us through the finished work of the Lamb. God never calls a man to any job or work, or to a ministry, for which He does not provide both the power and the grace. For when God calls you to a work, He makes full provision for it. The enthroned Christ is the guarantee of full and powerful provision. Whether it is that a person is called to be an apostle, or a prophet, or a pastor and teacher, or an evangelist, or maybe just a "help," it makes no difference. All the power and all the equipment for your service has been supplied by the enthroned Christ. Some people shun the gifts and the equipment that God provides, as if the gifts of the Spirit are in opposition to experiencing the Lord Jesus. One has often heard Christian believers say, "Jesus is enough for me, I do not need the gifts or equipment." The Word of God is clear; the gifts of the Holy Spirit are gifts of Christ. I would be very afraid if I needed an appendix operation and I met the surgeon and he told me his qualifications and I saw on the wall his certificates, and then he came to me with a hammer and a saw. He tells me the hammer is to knock me out, and the saw is to cut me open. When I protest, he asks me whether I would like to hear his qualifications again. I tell you I would not be so concerned about his high qualifications; I would want to know that he has also the right equipment for the operation.

All the gifts and the equipment we need for the work to which He has called us, have been provided for us through the finished work of the Lord Jesus, and made a reality in the person and the work of the Holy Spirit.

A FULL AND COMPLETE SALVATION

The third consequence is that the seated Christ is the guarantee of His finished work. There is nothing to be added to it; it is complete. He has provided us with a full salvation. The work of the Lord Jesus, which resulted in our salvation, is not just to do with having a "quiet time," a few moments of Bible reading and of prayer; or with just meeting other believers once a week. It is a question of union with God in Christ. It is as if a fusion has taken place between God and a saved human being in his or her human spirit. This discovery of the fullness and completeness of our salvation is all to do with personally knowing the Lord Jesus in a progressive way. For in Him God has given us everything. That salvation can turn a sinner into a saint, not only in position but in practical reality; for God is able through the Lord Jesus "to save to the uttermost."

In what I have written, there is no intention to give the impression that it is unimportant to read and study the Word of God, or to give time to prayer, or to meet with other believers. However we can make all these things "good works," and thus paralyze our progress in the knowledge of Him. Eternal life, in which everything for the Christian life and service is found, is the free gift of God. It is not earned. We have all seen a person who has been lost in sin and evil coming to the Lord Jesus, and spiritually steaming ahead of those of us who are many years older in the Lord. The reason is simple; that one has no claim on the Lord other than His grace. His or her basis for experiencing the fullness of their salvation is the finished work of the Lord Jesus.

God the Father has made the matter of our salvation so simple. We are saved because Jesus died in our place, and for no other reason. He then leads us to see that He has placed everything in Christ, and given Christ to us. In Him are all the blessings (see Ephesians 1:3); in Him God promises to meet every need according to His riches in glory (see Philippians 4:19); in Him is all the fullness and we are made full in Him (see Colossians 2:9-10); in Him are all the unsearchable riches (see Ephesians 3:8); in Him are all the treasures of wisdom and knowledge hidden (see Colossians 2:3).

Writing of God's eternal life, the Apostle John states: "He that hath the Son, hath the life" and continues: "... we are in Him that is true, even in His Son Jesus Christ. This is the true God, and eternal life" (1 John 5:12, 20).

The Apostle Paul declares: "He that spared not His own Son, but delivered Him up for us all, how shall He not also with Him freely give us all things?" (Romans 8:32).

It is no wonder to me that the Apostle Peter concludes his second letter with the words: "But grow in the grace and the knowledge of our Lord and Saviour Jesus Christ" (II Peter 3:18). The knowledge of which Peter speaks is not merely academic and impersonal book knowledge but is a living knowing of the Lord Himself.

Within this so great salvation everything has been given to us by the grace of God. Only one thing is expected of us, even demanded of us, and that is we follow Him fully and obey Him completely. Dear child of God, Jesus is seated, and the glorious meaning of His enthronement is that you and I have a salvation which is full and complete. Through this finished work all has been given to us freely. It has been given to us to appropriate, to enjoy, and to know in experience the full meaning of His life and riches.

SANCTIFICATION

The fourth consequence is that God the Father has given to the enthroned Lamb all who will be saved (see John 6:37, 39). The whole matter of our sanctification is centered in our being genuinely conformed to the likeness of God's Son, and it begins with us being "set apart."

At the heart of sanctification is this idea that we have been set apart. When we were born of the Spirit of God, whether we knew it or not, the Holy Spirit set us apart to the Lord, and for Him. The Lord Jesus commanded His disciples to go and make disciples of all nations; He did not command them to make converts but disciples. This is the great problem in Christendom and even amongst Evangelicals; we have many converts but few disciples. At the heart of our salvation is the idea that we have become saints by the grace of God alone. The word saint simply means "someone set apart." We were all lost sinners, some more bound and depraved than others, but God saved us through the finished work of the Lord Jesus. The New Testament calls such people saints. Unfortunately the normal idea of a saint is someone with huge sad eyes, pale and anaemic, and with a halo! If it does nothing else, it causes the normal believer to feel that he or she could never become a saint.

To set us apart, God has changed our position. He

has: "Delivered us from the domain of darkness and transferred us to the Kingdom of His beloved Son, in whom we have redemption, the forgiveness of sins" (Colossians 1:13-14 NASB). That is our divinely given position. He has set us apart for Himself. It is therefore a contradiction within itself, if a believer is not centered in the Lord Jesus. That person has a continuous civil war within his or her being; denying the very meaning of their redemption. Our God-given position is to be "set apart" for Him. From that point the Holy Spirit has to begin the work of turning our position into reality.

Many true believers feel that their circumstances, their problems, even their temperament, is not suited to be a saint! However when God saved you, he knew everything about you, and much more than you know. You have been "set apart" for the work that is to be done in you. God has made a supply of grace available to you, exactly commensurate with your circumstances, your problems and your temperament. Do not moan about them, but discover the grace! Then God will turn what is so terrible in your life into something that becomes the focal point of radiant glory. One day when you look back, you will say, "I would not have had it in any other way." You do not have to win the grace of God; it is already yours. You have to enter it by faith. Discover it and experience the grace of God which enables you to overcome the circumstances and the problems. Let the Holy Spirit make it the focal point of glory in your life.

To be sanctified is not to become heavy, dark, boring and colourless. We have all met people who are so super-spiritual but have no practical experience of the Lord! No one who is being conformed to the likeness of Christ feels that such work in them is being realized. It is others who recognise it. The person concerned often feels that they are hopeless and without spiritual character. The fact is, however, that the nearer we get to the Lord Jesus, the more we feel we are unlike Him. We should take great comfort from the fact that it is recorded in the Bible that often those who saw the Lord "fell down as one dead." God, by the Holy Spirit, is producing in us an incredible and eternal masterpiece, providing that we are devoted to the Lord and obedient to Him, and following Him whatever the cost may be. We may not feel that, but it is the fact!

THE HOUSE OF GOD

The fifth consequence is the building of the House of God. The Lord Jesus longs to see the House of God recovered, and built up, so that the top stone can be fitted into its place. Every thing required for the recovery of the Church, for the completion of its building, for it to be ready for the return of the Messiah, has been obtained in the finished work of the Lamb. The Lord Jesus made a plain and dogmatic statement when He said: "Upon this rock I will build my Church; and the gates of Hades shall not prevail against it" (Matthew 16:18). The seated Messiah is ruling in the midst of His enemies; the rod of His strength is going forth from Zion. It has very much to do with the building and completion of the Church. The foundation is laid; now the process of the building must take place. We have to grow into a holy temple in the Lord, a habitation of God in the Spirit. The enthroned Messiah is the architect and builder in this work and the Holy Spirit is the manager and supervisor in the practical accomplishment of it.

Tremendous forces are arraigned against this work! Satan and his host have marshalled all their forces to thwart the purpose of God. Nevertheless, he will fail! It is amazing how the Lord is so powerfully working in China, in Russia, in Eastern Europe, and elsewhere. Where Satan seemed to have triumphed, we hear of the vibrant and powerful work of the Holy Spirit.

Recently in the annual prayer conference of the Intercessors for Israel, it was uplifting to meet Chinese believers from mainland China, in particular from Sichuan and Beijing. They spoke of hundreds of thousands of believers under intense persecution, to whom numbers are being added by the day. Surely the blood of the martyrs once again has been the seed of the Church. We hear wonderful reports from Romania, Bulgaria, and Hungary of many coming to the Lord, and meeting together like the early Church. For me it was amazing to meet in another conference, six leaders of assemblies in Kazakhstan. They were all ex-Muslims, who had recently come to know the Lord. They said that they represented six assemblies of at least one thousand people in each assembly. All of this can only be the evidence that from the throne of the Messiah the Church is being built.

All through the history of the true Church, the enthroned Messiah has been watching over the building of it. The building has never stopped. Again and again the rod of His strength has gone forth from Zion, and the Holy Spirit has initiated new moves that have kept the Church alive and realigned it to His original purpose. It will be so to the coming of the Lord, for we have yet to see the Bride made ready for the Lord.

THE SALVATION OF ISRAEL

The sixth consequence of the Messiah being seated at the right hand of God, is that He is not only the little Lamb as slain in the midst of the throne, but also the Lion which is of the tribe of Judah, the Root of David. It is significant and noteworthy that the enthroned Messiah is introduced first as the Lion of Judah and then as the little Lamb which had been slain. From then on in the book of Revelation, He is called "The Lamb."

It is abundantly clear from the New Testament and from the clearest exposition of the Gospel within the Bible, the letter of the Apostle Paul to the Romans, that God intends finally to save the Jewish people. The words of the Apostle Paul are absolutely clear. No amount of spiritual acrobatics can make them say something different: "For I would not brethren have you be ignorant of this mystery, lest you be wise in your own conceits, that a hardening in part hath befallen Israel, until the fullness of the Gentiles be come in; and so all Israel shall be saved: Even as it is written, there shall come out of Zion the Deliverer; he shall turn away ungodliness from Jacob" (Romans 11:25-26).

In Psalm 110 God the Father says to the Lord Jesus that He will: "Send forth the rod of your strength out of Zion, rule thou in the midst of your enemies." It is inconceivable that the King of Israel, the King of the Jews, the King of Kings and Lord of Lords, should not use the rod of His strength for Israel, even though they are presently in unbelief and in rejection of the Messiah Jesus. Certainly He has done so already in Israel's recreation as a state and as a nation; in her re-gathering from over one hundred nations; and in her preservation and survival through at least ten wars in her modern history. That she was born out of the Holocaust, literally the ashes of her people, and at the weakest moment in her long history, is a divine miracle.

The story is unfinished! Israel is destined to become either a blessing or a curse to the nations. The defence, survival and triumph of Israel is totally due to the One whose rod of strength goes forth out of Zion. The enthronement of the Lion of Judah has enormous meaning and significance for modern Israel.

"He that keepeth Israel neither slumbers nor sleeps" (Psalm 121:4). There will come a day when all the suffering, persecution, hatred, and attempts at genocide, will turn to radiant glory! In the end, Israel will be gloriously saved! There could be no other result from the seated Lion of the Tribe of Judah, the Root and Offspring of David.

CAPTIVITY LED CAPTIVE

Another practical consequence of the Messiah's triumph is that captivity has been led captive. Ephesians 4:8 declares: "Wherefore he saith, 'When He ascended on high, he led captivity captive, and gave gifts unto men." "Captivity led captive" is the meaning and

31

consequence of the Lord Jesus being seated at the right hand of God the Father. He has ascended on high and is able to break every kind of imaginable bondage on the human scene. Now we have to face the fact that many of us, even though we are redeemed, are bound. We are like Lazarus—alive but still with the clothing of death binding our full and free movements. We are bound by inhibitions, by fear, and by various habits, and we long to be free. Sometimes we are even afraid to come out into the open and say, "I am bound." We feel it is as if one is saying, "I am not a Christian. I am not a believer." But there are times when the enemy does bind us, and there are other times when we have been bound all along and have never known it, until He touches us more deeply. Suddenly we are aware that we have a bondage within our lives, which we have lived with until that time. Then finally we want to be rid of it. But how do we get rid of it?

You can run all over the world for deliverance ministries; you can go to this place and to that place; run here and there, go to this meeting, or to that meeting; have this man lay his hands on you, or that man lay his hands on you; but you will never be free until you see that the guarantee of your freedom is the seated Christ. It is the Lord Jesus who has broken every form of captivity and bondage known to man. He has broken it, and you can enter into that freedom once you see with the eye of faith that the Lord Jesus, through His finished work, has led captivity captive. You can stand into what is your birthright in Him. Sometimes it needs the specialised ministry of certain brothers; sometimes it needs the prayer of the Church; it needs those wonderful words to be said over you: "You are free in the Name of the Lord." That is the ratification of something already done; but unless you yourself see it, you will never be free. It will come back to you like one of those dreadful weeds.

There is a plant called horseradish. It is a dreadful thing to have in your garden, although as a sauce it is very desirable. When you seek to pull it up, if you leave some of it in the ground, it multiplies ten times. If you destroy the whole root but leave a little bit, it will become another plant, a much stronger one. Some people's captivity is like that. They go to a meeting and say, "It is wonderful; I was delivered." But in a month's time they are found ten times as much in captivity; it has all returned again. What you need to see is that the Lord Jesus has broken all captivity. "You shall know the truth, and the truth shall make you free ... If therefore the Son shall make you free, you shall be free indeed" (John 8:32, 36 NASB).

INTERCESSION WHICH AVAILS

Another practical consequence is the powerful intercession of the Messiah. His intercession avails! Although it is not specifically stated, it seems that our Lord Jesus intercedes for us from His throne. For what does He intercede? He intercedes, that we may reach the goal of the Father. He points to His finished work and says, "Father, remember." How wonderful! It says, "He ever lives to make intercession for us." He has gone into heaven now to appear before the throne of God for us. What a guarantee we have! What glorious provision we have! We not only have an advocate with us on this earth, the Holy Spirit, but we have an advocate for us on the throne of God, the Lord Jesus. We will explore this subject of His intercession more fully in later chapters.

SATAN'S DAYS ARE NUMBERED

Satan's days are numbered and he knows it. It is another consequence. When Jesus sat down, it must have been like a sword that went through the being of Satan. If only the Messiah had stood to fight; if only He had continued fighting, but He sat down. Satan and the powers of darkness and evil know that His enthronement spells their final end. He knows that his time is up; he knows he has only a certain period of time, but he is so proud that he believes he can still win within that short time. We all know the pig-headedness of pride. People say to me, "If Satan knows that he is finished; why doesn't he give up?" It is because of pride. Pride is the most stubborn, obstinate, mulish, and blinding attribute in the whole world. Satan believes that he might yet win the day, but we know he cannot. Jesus is seated at God's right hand. He has won! The Messiah is now beyond the reach of Satan. Satan cannot dethrone Him, nor can he frustrate or thwart the Father's purpose for Him. The Lord Jesus has won and Satan's days are numbered! Every day that passes is one day less for the Devil.

THE OVERCOMES

Another marvelous consequence of the

enthronement of the Messiah is that through His finished work and His absolute triumph, He produces overcomers. "And they overcame him because of the blood of the Lamb, and because of the word of their testimony; and they loved not their life even unto death" (Revelation 12:11). This simply states the truth. Every overcomer overcomes Satan and his works, through the finished work of the Lord Jesus, through the blood of the Lamb! They overcome because with their mouths they confess the truth. It is the word of their testimony. They affirm and assert that Jesus is Lord and that He has won; that He is beyond the power of Satan to dethrone or to destroy; and that the Lamb's total victory has won for every child of God all that he or she needs to reach the throne of God. The basis for their overcoming is that they have let go of their self-life: They loved not their lives even unto death. Our problem is a universal one; it is the poison within our self-life. No one can overcome without allowing the Lord to deal with their self-life. We have to let it go. The Lord Jesus said: "Whosoever shall lose his life (soul or self-life: it is the Greek 'Psuche') for My sake and the gospel's shall save it" (Mark 8:35).

Any true believer, who by the grace of God is an overcomer, overcomes only by "the Overcomer" within them; it is Jesus. He said: "In Me ye may have peace. In the world ye have tribulation: but be of good cheer; I have overcome the world" (John 16:33b). Christ within us is the enabling force and power to overcome. There is no other.

JESUS WILL FILL ALL THINGS

We must state another and final consequence: Jesus, seated at the right hand of God the Father, is the guarantee that in the end the whole earth will be filled with Him. We have this wonderful little word in a parenthesis in Ephesians 4:9: "(Now this, He ascended, what is it but that he also descended into the lower parts of the earth? He that descended is the same also that ascended far above all the heavens, that He might fill all things)." He ascended far above the heavens that He might fill all things. In Ephesians it is said that the purpose of God is to sum up all things in Christ. He is to be in the end, the sum of everything! The guarantee of this is the enthroned Lamb, the seated Messiah.

There is something marvellous about the Father's words: "Until I make thine enemies thy footstool." The purpose of God from the beginning will then be fulfilled and Christ will have become the "sum of all things" (Ephesians 1:10).

However, the Apostle Paul in his first letter to the Corinthians has something further to add to this: "Then cometh the end, when He shall deliver up the kingdom to God, even the Father; when He shall have abolished all rule and all authority and power. For He must reign, till He hath put all His enemies under His feet. The last enemy that shall be abolished is death ... And when all things have been subjected unto Him, then shall the Son also Himself be subjected to Him (God the Father) that did subject all things unto Him, that God may be all in all" (I Corinthians 15: 24-26, 28). The whole cycle from the moment God had the idea of creating the universe, and the long parenthesis of the fall of man and of this planet, the Son has ended by His death at Calvary, by His glorious resurrection and ascension to God's right hand. His being seated is the expression of His complete triumph; and when He becomes the sum of all things, He hands the whole back to the Father, that God may be all in all.

Chapter 3

GOD'S ETERNAL PURPOSE—ZION

Psalm 110:1-3—The Lord saith unto my Lord, Sit thou at my right hand,
Until I make thine enemies thy footstool.
The Lord will send forth the rod of thy strength out of Zion:
Rule thou in the midst of thine enemies.

Father, we want to thank Thee that Thou hast already answered our prayer, and we believe that Thou hast made provision for us. And now, Lord, all we want to do, speaker and hearer alike, is to recognize our weakness and our utter dependence upon the gracious ministry of Thy Holy Spirit. But we do thank Thee that He has come to glorify the Lord Jesus and take of the things of the Lord Jesus and make them real to us. And we would look to Thee that in this time Thou will do just that. Give the spirit of quietness, Lord, we pray, and help us to hear Thy voice beyond the human voice, for we ask it in the name of our Lord Jesus. Amen.

ZION

In this chapter we shall consider the statement in Psalm 110:2: "The Lord will send forth the rod of thy strength out of Zion: Rule thou in the midst of thine enemies," and in particular the words, "out of Zion." Anyone who even superficially reads the Bible must come across the name "Zion" many times. For example, you read much about it when you read the Psalms, or Isaiah, or any of the other prophets. We are told that Zion is the delight of God; Zion is the dwelling place of God; Zion is the place which the Lord has chosen. Sometimes it is used of a particular mountain, Mount Zion, and other times it is used of a particular city, the city of Jerusalem. Furthermore, we find it mentioned not only in the Old Testament, but also in the New Testament. What does Zion signify? There are four things that I would like to underline in answer to this question.

MOUNT ZION

First of all, Zion refers to an actual mountain—Mount Zion. "Beautiful in elevation, the joy of the whole earth, is Mount Zion, on the sides of the north, the city of the great King" (Psalm 48:2).

Or again in II Samuel 5:7 we read the words: "Nevertheless David took the stronghold of Zion; the same is the city of David." Jerusalem is built on three mountains. God chose these three mountains, which together constitute a little plateau surrounded by higher mountains, in order that the people of God would not have a "high place" like the neighboring nations. These three mountains which constitute the city of Jerusalem are Mount Moriah, Mount Ophel, and Mount Zion. There are also three valleys, one to the west, the valley of the Hinnom; and one to the east, the valley of the Kidron. In the centre is a less steep but real valley, the Tyropoean valley (or the Cheese Makers valley). The Gentile nations normally chose the highest place on which to build an altar, or on which to build a temple. God chose three mountains all of them lower than the hills surrounding Jerusalem. Every one of those surrounding mountains—the Mount of Olives, Mount Scopus, French Hill, Ammunition Hill, Ramat, the Mount of Offense, the Mount of Evil Counsel, and Mount Gilo are all higher than the three He chose—Mount Zion, Mount Ophel, and Mount Moriah.

Zion is therefore a geographical place; a mountain upon which the city of Jerusalem was built; one mountain consisting of three hills. Mount Zion was the name which in the end came to represent all three. For example: "Mount Zion ... the city of the great king" (Psalm 48:2). "David took the stronghold of Zion; the same is the city of David" (II Samuel 5:7).

THE CITY OF JERUSALEM

Secondly, Zion came to mean the city of David or the city of Jerusalem. Consider Psalm 48:1: "Great is the Lord, and greatly to be praised, in the city of our God, in his holy mountain. Beautiful in elevation, the joy of the whole earth, is Mount Zion, on the sides of the north, the city of the great King."

Verse 12: "Walk about Zion, and go round about her; number the towers thereof; mark ye well her bulwarks; consider her palaces: that ye may tell it to the generation following." In other words, it was a city. So often when we read of Zion, it is not just the actual mountain, but it speaks of Jerusalem, the city of our God, the city of the great King.

NATIONAL AND POLITICAL ZION

Thirdly, there is another manner in which we should consider this word Zion, and that is the national and political. Now here we come into a controversial area, but in my estimation there is a national and political significance to the way the Scripture uses the word Zion. For instance, we discover that which we call "Zionism" in Psalm 137 describes the spirit of national and political Zionism.

"By the rivers of Babylon, there we sat down, yea, we wept, when we remembered Zion. Upon the willows in the midst thereof we hanged up our harps. For there they that led us captive required of us songs, and they that wasted us required of us mirth, saying, sing us one of the songs of Zion. How shall we sing the Lord's song in a foreign land? If I forget thee, O Jerusalem, let my right hand forget her skill, let my tongue cleave to the roof of my mouth, if I remember thee not; if I prefer not Jerusalem above my chief joy" (Psalm 137:1-6).

The heart of what we call Zionism is basically described by this Psalm; it is the longing of the Jewish people for their homeland, and for the recreation of the Jewish State as a sovereign state among the states of the world.

It is prophesied in Isaiah 59:20: "And a Redeemer will come to Zion, and unto them that turn from transgression in Jacob, saith the Lord."

The Apostle Paul quotes this when he declared: "For I would not, brethren, have you ignorant of this mystery, lest ye be wise in your own conceits, that a hardening in part hath befallen Israel, until the fullness of the Gentiles be come in; and so all Israel shall be saved: even as it is written, 'There shall come out of Zion the Deliverer; He shall turn away ungodliness from Jacob" (Romans 11:25-26).

By the Spirit of God, Paul states that this is going to be fulfilled after the reconstitution of the Jewish people as a sovereign nation among the nations. The nation was born in a day, on the 14th May 1948. In a single day the nation was recreated after two thousand years of exile and wandering. That however is the political and national, but far more than that is predicted. When the veil on the Jewish heart is taken away, there will be a great turning to the Lord. The prophet Zechariah speaks about this when he says: "They shall look unto me whom they have pierced; and they shall mourn for him as one mourneth for an only son, and shall be in bitterness for him, as one is in bitterness for his firstborn." This will be the result of the: "Spirit of grace and supplication being poured upon the House of David and the inhabitants of Jerusalem" (Zechariah 12:10). The prophet continues and predicts that the whole nation will mourn—every family, husbands and wives apart.

Anyone who knows anything about Jewish burial customs will know that there are seven days of absolute mourning from the death, in which the whole of normal life is disrupted. Then there is a further one month in which life is seriously abnormal. This is followed by one year in which life is still not normal. What Zechariah was prophesying was not an event that would take place in a single day but over at least a month or even a year.

Now that means that the Word of God prophesies that there will come, in the end, the most incredible miracle in Jewish history, especially in Israel. There will be a movement of the Spirit of God through which the Jewish people will recognise, as no other nation has in the history of the nations, the significance of their history in the light of Jesus. The Messiah Jesus, was born King of the Jews; He died the King of the Jews, and there has never been another Davidic Jewish King, until He returns whose right it is to take the throne.

The most wonderful thing is that when that day comes, the Bible states it will be "life from the dead." So I have a great argument with people who tell me that Zionism is merely a political movement and has nothing to do with the Word of God. Whether we like it or not, whatever may be the failings of political Zionism as a movement, God's Word predicted it. There would have been no recreated Nation of Israel apart from Zionism. According to the Word of God the recreation of the State of Israel is by the hand of God, amazingly in their unbelief. We find therefore in a number of places certain references in the Scriptures to Zion, which seem to have a national and political meaning, but the end will be spiritual.

The prophet Jeremiah declares: "Hear the word of the Lord, O ye nations and declare it in the isles afar off; and say, He that scattered Israel will gather him, and keep him, as a shepherd doth his flock. For the Lord hath ransomed Jacob, and redeemed him from the hand of him that was stronger than he. And they shall come and sing in the height of Zion, and shall flow unto the goodness of the Lord, to the grain, and to the new wine, and to the oil, and to the young of the flock and of the herd: and their soul shall be as a watered garden; and they shall not sorrow any more at all. Then shall the virgin rejoice in the dance, and the young men and the old together; for I will turn their mourning into joy, and will comfort them, and make them rejoice from their sorrow ... And there is hope for thy latter end, saith the Lord; and thy children shall come again to their own border" (Jeremiah 31:10-13, 17). So much of this prophecy has been marvelously fulfilled in our day, but more is awaiting its fulfillment. We can be sure that there are spiritual lessons to be gained from these verses, but there is also the geographical, national and even political meaning.

ETERNAL AND SPIRITUAL ZION

The fourth and most important meaning of all is the eternal and the spiritual. This is where the Word of God takes Zion, the actual mount and the city of Jerusalem, and invests it with eternal and spiritual significance. Here we come to the heart of the matter.

Consider the manner in which the Lord speaks of Jerusalem: "The mighty One, God, the Lord, hath spoken, and called the earth from the rising of the sun unto the going down thereof. Out of Zion, the perfection of beauty, God hath shined forth. Our God cometh, and doth not keep silence ... Gather my saints together unto me, those that have made a covenant with me by sacrifice" (Psalm 50:1-3a, 5a). Has Jerusalem in her history ever been the "perfection of beauty?"

Even when Solomon's temple was there in all its glory, Jerusalem was still a flea-bitten place. It could not be compared with Babylon! Babylon with its magnificent boulevards; its wonderful avenues; its great canals bringing ships up hundreds of miles from the Persian Gulf; its great hanging botanical and zoological gardens that were famed throughout the ancient world; its stock exchange, and postal system and much else. Babylon was glorious, while Jerusalem had none of the normal attributes by which a capital city is usually chosen.

What was Jerusalem? All the famous capitals of the world are built on major crossroads, or on large natural harbors, or upon great rivers that are navigable, but not Jerusalem. She is not built on any crossroads. The main trade routes of the ancient world ran either sixty miles east, the King's Highway, or forty miles west, the Way of the Sea, the Via Maris. There is no large natural harbor in Jerusalem, and no river to write about. The only rivers were the Kidron, which was nothing more than a small winter stream, and the Hinnom that was another small winter stream. The River Jordan, approximately thirty miles east of Jerusalem, could be swallowed up even by the river Thames, which in turn could be swallowed up by a whole number of North American rivers; not to mention the huge Asian, African and South American rivers! Even Jerusalem's water supply was originally outside of the city walls, the spring Gihon, and was only brought within the city walls by King Hezekiah. Who would have chosen a city as its capital without its own water supply within its walls? God chose Jerusalem and thus catapulted it into history! He chose it because its very survival depended upon His protection and His faithfulness, and not on its own resources.

Note carefully the words: "Out of Zion ... God hath shined forth." It was the shining forth of God through this city that is its greatness. Zion, Jerusalem, was chosen by God to represent Himself on this fallen earth, to represent His eternal purpose, His Word, His throne, His Messiah, His redeemed, and His Kingdom. Zion is a symbol of an eternal and divine reality. It expresses something deep within the heart of God, something, as it were, in His mind. In this sense it is "the perfection of beauty." Before ever He created the universe, before He created man, He had in His heart something that we now call Zion, the City of God, the dwelling place of God.

In the Hebrew letter we find these words: "But ye are come unto mount Zion, and unto the city of the living God, the heavenly Jerusalem, and to innumerable hosts of angels, to the general assembly and Church of the firstborn who are enrolled in heaven" (Hebrews 12:22-23a). Those who have been redeemed by the blood of the Lamb have come to Mount Zion. What Mount Zion? Most of the redeemed have never even been to the physical Mount Zion; their feet have never stood upon the soil or the dust of Mount Zion. What then? What does it mean that you are come unto Mount Zion to the city of the living God? Just to confuse us further, it says in chapter 13:14: "For we have not here an abiding city, but we seek after the city which is to come." Now how does the writer contradict himself? First, he tells us we are in the city, and then he says we are not there yet. What is he writing about?

Again, when we come to Revelation 21:2-5a it says, "And I saw the holy city, new Jerusalem, coming down out of heaven from God, made ready as a bride adorned for her husband. And I heard a great voice out of the throne saying, Behold, the tabernacle of God is with men, and he shall dwell with them, and they shall be his peoples, and God himself shall be with them, and be their God: and he shall wipe away every tear from their eyes; and death shall be no more; neither shall there be mourning, nor crying, nor pain, any more; the first things are passed away. And he that sitteth on the throne said, Behold, I make all things new."

Every child of God knows that we are not there yet. Nevertheless our whole life as believers, our whole life as the people of God, the Church, is bounded by that City. By the finished work of the Lamb we have arrived and yet we are arriving.

THE HIGHWAYS TO ZION IN OUR HEART

Dear people of God, here we come home. When we come to the spiritual and eternal, then every one of us must surely know that this has everything to do with us. If you are redeemed, if you are saved and born of the Spirit of God, then you have come to Zion. First of all, you have come to Zion, and Zion is in you. By your new birth something has happened whether you know it or not! The fact of the matter is that you have come to Zion and Zion is in you. You only need someone like me to sing a song or to say a few words, and it truly awakens chords in you that you may never have thought were there. Deep within every redeemed human heart, the highways to Zion have been implanted. We may not know it, we may not understand it, it may have been smothered by institutionalism, organisationalism, or denominationalism, or whatever else you like to call it; but within our hearts, by our new birth, the highways to Zion have been implanted in us. We have come to Zion and Zion has come into us.

Let us move a little deeper into this whole matter. "The Lord will send forth the rod of thy strength out of Zion." What does this mean? Where is our Lord enthroned at this very moment? He is seated at the right hand of God the Father. What does it mean then that the Lord will send forth the rod of His strength out of Zion? It must mean that this spiritual reality involves us in the heavenlies. It encompasses the right hand of God and this fallen earth itself. Every born again child of God has been brought into a union with God, which means that we are in heavenly places in Christ, and at the same time on this fallen earth.

God the Father declared to the Messiah that He would: "Send forth the rod of thy strength out of Zion." The simple fact is that the enthroned Messiah is seated in Zion and that from Zion He will rule in the midst of His enemies! This spiritual and eternal Zion is the place where

the throne of God is, and the enthroned Lamb is to be found. This is confirmed by the inspired words of the Psalmist: "Yet I have set my King upon my holy hill of Zion" (Psalm 2:6).

Years ago when I was in my early teens, newly saved,

I heard a speaker preach on this very kind of subject and I could not understand a word of what he said. But one thing he spoke at the end, which I have never forgotten: "Some of you will not understand what I am talking about, but I feel like a spiritual tourist guide. I am taking you up in a cable car to a high point and showing you distant horizons. You will never be the same again."

As you read this, may you never be the same again. A kind of holy discontent is the greatest thing to spur one on to know the Lord. Did not the Lord say it: "Blessed are they that hunger and thirst after righteousness: for they shall be filled" (Matthew 5:6).

Zion the Home of God

In one of the songs of ascents there is a declaration: "For the Lord hath chosen Zion; he hath desired it for his habitation. This is my resting-place for ever: here will I dwell; for I have desired it" (Psalm 132:13-14). What is a habitation? It is a rather old fashioned word! We could say "dwelling place" or even better "home." The Lord has chosen Zion; He has desired it for His home. Twice the Lord uses the word "desired it," meaning that we are dealing with something of tremendous importance to the Lord Himself. Somewhere in eternity past, before ever a single star was flung into place, before ever this planet was set spinning on its course, before ever man was created and the breath of God was breathed into him, far back in eternity past in the heart of God there was a desire. What was that desire? It was to have a people that could come into a union with Himself, a people that could become partakers of His divine nature, a people that could, as it were, be His home. God does not dwell in forests and lakes and in the sky or in the air, although He certainly visits them, and His presence can be found there. God does not dwell in houses made with bricks and stones and wood, although again we can meet Him in a house or a building. God dwells in a home of redeemed human beings. The purpose of God from the very beginning was to make human beings His home. He created mankind with a capacity for Himself; human beings, who in partaking of the tree of life, would enter into a union with Himself.

It would have been wonderful if there had been no fall! It is even more wonderful, however, that He sent His Son into this world to undo the fall, to bear away the sin of the world, and to open the gate back to God. He did this in order that the most depraved and hopeless sinner might be washed in the blood of the Lamb. Such sinners, loosed from their sins, joined to God through Jesus Christ, and made heirs of God and joint heirs with Jesus the Messiah, are the eternal dwelling place of God.

Do you understand this amazing thought in the heart of God? Do you really realize what it means? If we began to glimpse a little of it, we would suddenly realize one simple but marvelous fact: our salvation is not an end, but a means to an end. It is not the "all" of God; it is the beginning, the instrument of God. It is the means by which God takes a fallen humanity, sinful, depraved, alienated, and lost, and brings them back into His original purpose, back into His Zion.

Sometimes people say, "Why didn't God wash His hands of the whole thing and start again?" It is, however, a cause for tremendous marveling and worship, that God never gave up but found a way to take rebellious people like us, who, when we are saved, are a load of trouble to Him, and opened a way for us to come back to Him. If we were trouble before we were saved, we have certainly been trouble since we were saved! For all of us Christ has given up Himself and opened the way back to God, but He has never been diverted from His original purpose. The fall of man has not destroyed the original purpose of God or nullified it. It has actually become a greater glory, for now we have people who were lost in sin and darkness, torn out from the powers of darkness, delivered from them, and transferred into the kingdom of His dear Son. Only He could have done that!

In every truly born again believer, at the moment of their spiritual birth, the highways to Zion are implanted. The day you were born of God and saved, whether you knew it or not, something in you opened up to a new creation, to a new world, to the Eternal Purpose of God. Maybe it was smothered very quickly because you were never taught, or instructed, or helped. Or maybe through your own sin or disobedience it was lost. Nevertheless, those highways to Zion are there within your heart. May you rediscover them through the reading of this book.

THE FOUNDATION OF THE HOUSE

Have you ever noticed the remarkable words

contained in Isaiah 8:14: "And he (The one called Immanuel is referred to three times in chapter seven and eight.) shall be for a sanctuary; but for a stone of stumbling and for a rock of offence to both the houses of Israel, for a gin and for a snare to the inhabitants of Jerusalem. And many shall stumble thereon, and fall, and be broken, and be snared, and be taken."

What an extraordinary word! "He shall be for a sanctuary and a stone of stumbling." Either He is the House of God, the Temple of God, the Habitation of God, or He becomes the very wreckage of everything. Either you fall over Him, trip over Him, or you find in Him the whole Eternal Purpose of God.

THE BUILDING

Another wonderful Scripture is Isaiah 28:16: "Therefore thus saith the Lord God, Behold, I lay in Zion for a foundation a stone, a tried stone, a precious corner-stone of sure foundation: he that believeth shall not be in haste." `

Dear child of God, what does it mean "Behold, I lay in Zion for a foundation a stone, a tried stone, a precious corner-stone of sure foundation"? What is the point of having a foundation if you do not have a building? What is the point of having a cornerstone if there is no structure on the foundation? The whole point is this: Jesus our Immanuel is the sanctuary of God; He is the foundation, the cornerstone, the headstone, and the top stone. All these stones are quarried out of the same material—His nature and His life. This is that to which God has called you. If you have been saved, your feet have been put on a sure foundation. Are you aware of it? (see 1 Corinthians 11:3)

Most believers would say that the Lord Jesus is their only salvation and their only foundation. What is the point however of having a foundation if there is no building? Supposing we were to have a conference in a university auditorium in some city, and we all came together to meet there, and we discover that we only have a foundation. We are to sit on the concrete floor of the foundation; there are no seats, no walls, no roof, no lights, and no amenities. What would you think? You would at least think that those who organized this conference ought to see a doctor! The fact of the matter is that every one knows a foundation is only the beginning. In building a house, the first vital and essential matter is to lay the foundation, then the cornerstone on the foundation, and then the whole building. The purpose of a foundation is the building.

"He shall be for a sanctuary." He is the Foundation, the Cornerstone, the Headstone and the Top stone. He is the beginning and the end. The apostle Peter takes this up when he quotes these words: "Unto whom coming, a living stone, rejected indeed of men, but with God elect, precious, ye also, as living stones, are built up a spiritual house, to be a holy priesthood, to offer up spiritual sacrifices, acceptable to God through Jesus Christ" (I Peter 2:4-5).

In Ephesians 2:20 the Apostle Paul also seems to be referring to these Scriptures: "Being built upon the foundation of the apostles and prophets, Christ Jesus himself being the chief corner stone; in whom the whole building, fitly framed together, groweth into a holy temple in the Lord; in whom ye also are builded together for a home of God in the Spirit."

In these Scriptures we are dealing with God's eternal purpose. What was that purpose? It was to have a home. It was to bring people who are born of His Spirit, saved by His grace, and washed in the blood of the Lamb, onto that foundation which is Jesus Christ and relate them to one another in Him. It was to build them together, to fitly frame them together, and to cause them to grow into a holy temple in the Lord. But where do we find such understanding, let alone such experience?

BORN IN ZION

Listen to these amazing words: "His foundation is in the holy mountains. The Lord loveth the gates of Zion more than all the dwellings of Jacob. Glorious things are spoken of thee, O city of God. I will make mention of Rahab (Egypt) and Babylon as among them that know me: behold, Philistia, and Tyre, with Ethiopia: this one was born there." (Where? This one was born in Zion.) "Yea, of Zion it shall be said, This one and that one were born in her; and the Most High himself will establish her. The Lord will count, when he writeth up the peoples, this one was born there" (Psalm 87).

Are you born of God? When God writes up the peoples, when He takes stock, as it were, He will say, "This one was not born in Europe or in the United Kingdom or in Africa, or in China; this one was born in

Zion." When God writes up all the people, it is of paramount importance to Him where they were born. Are they of the earth, earthy? Or have they been born of Zion? And this is exactly what the Apostle Paul says in Galatians 4:26: "But the Jerusalem that is above is free, which is our mother." Every citizen of the Jerusalem that is above has had a second birth.

You have a mother, and your mother is Jerusalem; you have been born a free man, a free woman. You have not been born under Law or under bondage; you have been born free because you have been born of the Jerusalem which is above.

In Psalm 87:6-7 it says: "The Lord will count, when he writeth up the peoples, this one was born there. They that sing as well as they that dance shall say, All my fountains are in thee."

THE PLACE WHERE HIS NAME DWELLS

The Lord declares: "Ye shall not do so unto the Lord your God. But unto the place which the Lord your God shall choose out of all your tribes, to put his name there, even unto his habitation shall ye seek, and thither thou shalt come; and thither ye shall bring your burnt-offerings, and your sacrifices, and your tithes, and the heave-offering of your hand, and your vows, and your freewill-offerings, and the firstlings of your herd and of your flock: and there ye shall eat before the Lord your God. And again He says: "Then it shall come to pass that to the place which the Lord your God shall choose to cause his name to dwell there, thither shall ye bring all that I command you" (Deuteronomy 12:4-7a, 11).

These are two of a number of the occurrences in which the Lord introduces Jerusalem as "The place where I have caused My Name to dwell." The Lord's extraordinary description of Jerusalem has to arrest our attention. One looks in vain for another example of a city being described by God in this manner. It is unique! What then is the significance of this Divine description?

Names in the Bible tend to be prophetic: they describe the personality, the nature, and the character of a person; their calling and their work. Names are not given for how the name sounds, but they are given with significant and often prophetic meaning. When the Lord says that Jerusalem is "the place where I have caused My Name to dwell," it means simply that the city represents the being and the character of God; it expresses His mind and His heart, it signifies His throne, His Word, His purpose, His Messiah, His redemption, and His redeemed. For this reason Jerusalem stands today where she has ever stood, whilst many other powerful cities contemporary with her, have disappeared. She is as eternal as God, and will not disappear until that Jerusalem which is above descends.

God said to the children of Israel: "You are not to bring your free will offerings or your sacrifices, or your tithes, or anything else, to any city, or town, or place that you shall choose, but you shall come to the place where I have caused my Name to dwell, even my home." Now that place is Jerusalem, His dwelling place, His habitation.

What does the New Covenant have to say about this? Where is the "place" God has caused His name to dwell? It is Jesus. Is that not so? "Neither is there salvation in any other for there is none other name given under heaven whereby we must be saved."

Or again in Matthew 18:20 the Lord Jesus declares, "For where two or three are gathered together in My Name, there am I in the midst of them."

Or in John 15:4-5 it says: "Abide in Me, and I in you … For apart from me ye can do nothing."

One of the most revealing phrases in the New Testament is the little phrase, "in Christ." It explains everything. In Christ you have salvation; in Christ you have eternal life; in Christ you find the power of God, the exceeding greatness of His power; in Christ you have all the treasures of wisdom and knowledge hidden; in Christ you have all the unsearchable riches of God; in Christ you have unfathomable resources; in Christ you have everything! All the blessings are in Christ, all the provision of God is in Christ, all the life of God is in Christ, all the gifts of God are in Christ; God the Father has given everything in Christ.

What do the words mean "in my name"? Many people think of it as a little charm that is added to the end of a prayer. It is not wrong to say at the end of our prayer: "in the Name of the Lord Jesus," but we must understand what we are saying. Do we use it as a little magical charm or do we understand what we are saying when we pray in His Name, or we meet in His Name, or we act in His Name? It means that we are in Him; we are members of His body.

My name is Lance Lambert. I have a head: Lance Lambert is my head and also my body and the members of my body share my name. If I stretch out my hand, it is in the name of Lance Lambert. If my feet step forward, it is in the name of Lance Lambert. If I knock something over, my hand or my foot did it, not my head, but it is in the name of Lance Lambert. My body lives in the name of Lance Lambert. It is not living in someone else's name. Everything I do is in the name of Lance Lambert. From my big toe to my little finger, it is all in the name of Lance Lambert.

It fills us with awe when the true meaning of the Name dawns on us. God has placed us, positioned us in Christ! He has made us members of Christ and members one of another. We have become members of the body of the Lord Jesus so that the Name of Jesus has been named on us.

In the early days, part of the understanding of baptism was that the Name of the Lord Jesus was named upon you; you were named with His Name. You shall not offer your freewill offerings, or your sacrifices, or your peace offerings, or whatever else, in any place that you shall choose. You shall come to the place which I have chosen to cause My Name to dwell, my home, Christ. There in Christ you shall meet God and hear God; and you shall serve God.

In Christ everything, out of Christ nothing; in Christ blessing, out of Christ tension; in Christ joy, out of Christ misery; in Christ power, out of Christ paralysis. Oh, what an epitaph this is for much Christian work! So much of it is outside of Christ. It is done in the Name of Christ, but it is not done out of the life and power which is in Christ. May the Lord enable us to remain, to abide in

Christ, and there in Him discover all that we could ever need.

Chapter 4

THE NECESSITY OF LEARNING TO REIGN WITH CHRIST

Psalm 110:1-3—The Lord saith unto my Lord, Sit thou at my right hand,
Until I make thine enemies thy footstool.
The Lord will send forth the rod of thy strength out of Zion:
Rule thou in the midst of thine enemies.
Thy people offer themselves willingly
In the day of thy power, in the beauty of holiness."

Oh Father, we have already committed ourselves to Thee and opened our hearts to Thee, but as we turn to Thy word, I just want to confess my own need of that anointing that is in the Lord Jesus. And oh Father, whether for speaker or for hearer we all need that anointing provided for every one of us in our Lord Jesus. For it says that oil runs down the head upon the beard right down to the hem of the garment. Lord, we would ask Thee to make this time to be just like that, gloriously enabled by Thy divine power so that we meet with Thee and receive from Thee. And we shall give to Thee all the praise and the glory in the name of our Lord Jesus. Amen.

In the last chapter we considered The Eternal Purpose of God as centered in Zion. We come now to the next important truth; it is the headship and authority of the Messiah over and through His own. This truth is simple but challenging; it is that those He redeems should learn now, on this present fallen earth, how to reign with Him.

The Apostle Paul writes: "And what the exceeding greatness of His power to us-ward who believe, according to that working of the strength of His might, which he wrought in Christ, when He raised Him from the dead, and made Him to sit at His right hand in the heavenly places, far above all rule, and authority, and power, and dominion, and every name that is named, not only in this world but also in that which is to come: and He put all things in subjection under His feet and gave Him to be head over all things to the Church, which is His body, the fullness of Him that filleth all in all … even when we were dead through our trespasses, made us alive together with Christ(by grace have ye been saved), and raised us up with Him, and made us to sit with Him in the heavenly places in Christ Jesus: that in the ages to come …" (Ephesians 1:19-23 2:5-7).

In these words Paul, inspired by the Spirit of God, states that we are the body of Christ, the fullness of Him who fills everything in everyone. He then goes on to write that God the Father has made us alive together with Christ, raised us up with Him, and made us to sit with Him in heavenly places. Is this the present position of the Church, and of the individual believer, now to be experienced on this earth, or something only relating to the future? It is astounding to think that Christ has been made, by His ascension and enthronement, "Head over all things to the Church which is His body." Carefully note that God puts all things "in subjection under His feet." We have many enemies facing us; there are seemingly insoluble problems; circumstances that are satanic; strongholds of darkness and evil which refuse to budge. Can it be true that these matters are part of those things subjected under His feet, over which He has been made Head? Or do we have to be bound by them, looking upon them as immovable and invincible? After all, it is the enthroned Messiah Jesus at the right hand of God, who is the truly immovable and invincible One!

MADE TO SIT WITH CHRIST IN HEAVENLY PLACES

Furthermore, the Apostle Paul underlines this truth by stating that God has: "Made us to sit in heavenly places in Christ Jesus" (Ephesians 2:6). Carefully note again: "Made us to sit ... in Christ Jesus;" and again: "in heavenly places." Is this a fairy tale? An ideal, which it is impossible for us to experience or to realize at present on this fallen earth? It would be incredible if the apostle was hoodwinking us! It is surely clear that he means exactly what he says! Joined to Christ by the Holy Spirit, we have been made to sit with Him. To make it even more clear, it is in "heavenly places" that we are made to sit in Christ Jesus. Spiritually, we are to share the absolute triumph of the Lord Jesus. Once the eyes of our hearts are illuminated by the Spirit of God, and we see this fact, we face the problems, the conflict, the turmoil, and even the satanic intrigues, in an altogether different light.

Some have taken this truth in such an extreme

manner, as to go completely overboard. They believe that we can Christianize the whole world system; its social, educational, scientific, economic and even political order. In my estimation this takes the truth to such an extreme that it becomes error! For those who believe this, they understand that the Church is to take the whole world and finally, when it is Christianized, to offer it to the Lord Jesus, who will then return. It is absolutely true that all through the history of the living Church, the world has been impacted, even changed by the light which has shone through the believers. Biblical principles have become the foundation of national life and many evil practices banished, as for e.g. in The United States and Canada, The United Kingdom, and various European and Scandinavian nations.

It is however also true, that when the Church has ignored the Great Commission, and turned inwards, its light has become darkness and its salt has become ineffective. The consequences have been disastrous for the Church and for believers. The world has entered the Church, and made it a human society, as worldly and as earthly minded as fallen humanity; and often it became the persecutor of faithful believers.

DISCERNING THE WILL OF THE HEAD

However, the truth lies between these two extremes. It is obvious in the Word of God that the Church cannot and must not be passive and inactive. When she is in living union with the Head enthroned at the right hand of God, anything is possible. It is the Headship and Lordship of Jesus, which is the key to the effectiveness of both the Church and the individual believer in this world. It is the spiritual ability to discern the will and mind of the Head, which makes all the difference; to have an ear to hear what He is saying, and the faith to obey Him implicitly,.

It is unambiguously clear from the Word of God that the Lamb is enthroned and has won the battle. He is not fighting but seated! The situation of His body on earth is different. Satan and his host know very well that Jesus has won, and it is because of this fact that in this present age, and on this earth, they attack the Church and the true believer. Although joined to Christ, and seated in Him, the environment of this world is anything but peaceful. The Lord Jesus has said: "In Me ye may have peace. In the world ye have tribulation" (John 16:33). We are also told that: "Through many tribulations we must enter into the Kingdom of God" (Acts 14:22).

PUTTING ON THE WHOLE ARMOR OF GOD

The Apostle Paul is lucid and clear concerning the war that we are in when he says: "Put on the whole armor of God, that ye may be able to stand against the wiles of the devil. For our wrestling is not against flesh and blood, but against the principalities, against the powers, against the world-rulers of this darkness, against the spiritual hosts of wickedness in the heavenly places. Wherefore, take up the whole armor of God ..." (Ephesians 6:11-13).

Such armor is needed only for conflict and war! Ephesians marks the high tide of revelation in the New Testament, and it is significant that the apostle concludes his letter with the fact that the Church in Ephesus, and probably also in Laodicea, was in a spiritual war situation, in spite of the enthroned Lamb. We need to note carefully that Paul tells us to stand in the full armor, to withstand, and having done all to stand. In other words we are to stand in the complete triumph of the enthroned Messiah, and the fact that with Him nothing is impossible. Whilst the Church in Ephesus stood in the full revealed will of God, they would win; they would be as immovable and invincible as He, even when they paid the ultimate price in physical death and martyrdom.

TRAINING HIS PEOPLE FOR GOVERNMENT

The desire of God is not only that we should be born of Him, and be His children, but that we should grow up, be trained, educated, disciplined and qualified to be part of His government and of His administration. It does not just mean that willy-nilly every single child of God is going to sit on a throne! The Scripture is quite clear on this matter. It says, "If we suffer with Him we shall also reign with Him" (II Timothy 2:12 AV). There is an if here. If we are not prepared for the discipline of the Holy Spirit on this earth, or for the discipline of the Church and of our brothers and sisters, we will disqualify ourselves from eternal government. We are dealing with a very important matter. It is remarkable that in this Psalm, divinely inspired by the Spirit of God, but humanly speaking written by David, we have the heart of God coming down to us from thousands of years ago.

The Lord's first words to man in Genesis 1:28 were: "And they shall have dominion." God's idea for man was that first he should subdue the earth, cultivate and till it, watching over it and administering it. He was to have dominion over the whole earth. The Garden of Eden was to be the kindergarten. All the physical and natural side would be in that kindergarten, in which man would be trained in union with God to have dominion. From there he would have gone on to the spiritual dimension, ruling as it were with God. However man fell, but God's purpose has not changed. From the very beginning His desire has been to find His home amongst us, to build us up together, to fitly frame us together, and to bring us into a relationship with one another not merely for time but for eternity. His plan was always to train us for the throne.

It will be worth all the afflictions, the trials, the routine trivia of Church life, the collisions and all the corners which have to be knocked off in the House of God, to be part of that New Jerusalem. It will be worthwhile to have walked the way of the cross, to have laid down one's life for one's brothers and sisters, if in the end we come to the throne of God. Could there be anything more breathtaking in the whole world than finally to come to the center of God's purpose for man; to be at the very end, by the grace of God alone, right at the heart of what God had first desired for man; to have reached the goal of our salvation, which is that we should reign with Him!

LEARNING TO APPROPRIATE THE GRACE OF GOD

No person will ever come to the throne unless first they learn how in the Name of the Lord to rule over their own circumstances; to reign over their own problems, inherited perhaps from family, or from other sources which have had nothing to do with them. We have to learn how to appropriate the grace of God, and how to overcome. For God has said we shall not be the tail but the head. "The Lord will make thee the head, and not the tail; and thou shalt be above only, and thou shalt not be beneath" (Deuteronomy 28:13). Most of us are "beneath" and not above. We have to learn that God has provided all the grace required and necessary for us to reign with Christ here and now. For some of us our training ground will be the kitchen sink; it will be all the routine duties of home and family. For others it will be college, or hospital work, or the factory bench. For yet others it will be business life. For all of us who are redeemed, it will be Church life and the many problems we face in it.

People are always looking for the perfect Church; they are looking for a Church without problems. What is wrong with us? We do not want a Church without problems; we want a Church with problems, for that is where we are taught to overcome. If we are going to have one of those lovely places where all is praise and joy, and where there is never a collision, never a disagreement, or a ripple of difficulty, how are we to learn?

We can live in a fool's paradise and never need to learn to appropriate the grace of God; or to learn how to maintain the unity of the Spirit; or to lay down our self-life for our brothers and sisters. In the Church on earth there is much that is dirty and filthy. How does all this dirt and scum come to the surface if it is not in our being built together? It all begins to come to the top, and it is at that point that we can become annoyed and irritated with one another and say, "Farewell, I will find something else more spiritual than this lot." But if you opt out of a company of God's children gathering on the genuine foundation of Christ, you have opted out of training for eternal government. You have disqualified yourself from the school of Christ, from the school of the Holy Spirit; for the Lord is seeking to train us to appropriate the grace of God, the power of God, and the anointing which is ours in the Holy Spirit, and thus overcome these problems.

THE WAY GOD DEALS WITH MOUNTAINS

God does not always remove problems! It is interesting to note that in the Word of God there are four ways in which God deals with mountains. In the Bible mountains often symbolize difficulties and obstacles—the matters that stand between us and the fulfillment of God's purpose.

One way he deals with them is that He causes them to melt. "O that thou wouldest rend the heavens, that thou wouldest come down, that the mountains might flow down at thy presence" (Isaiah 64:1 mg). What a wonderful experience it is when you have a mountain of problem or difficulty, and suddenly the Lord steps in, and the whole mountain disappears overnight. Oh, how we praise the Lord!

Then there is another way in which God deals with mountains; He gives us faith to remove them. We say to the mountain: "Be thou removed in the Name of the Lord," and it is removed (see Matthew 17:20-21). What a great excitement that is when that happens!

Then there is yet another way God deals with mountains; He leaves them. Some people say, "That is not possible with the Lord." The Lord however declares: "I will make all My mountains a way" (Isaiah 49:11). In other words, the mountains are left in place, but they become the way of the Lord; they have become a highway of God. He has made the problems and difficulties a way for you to travel, so that instead of them destroying you, or paralyzing you, in fact you traverse them and see the purpose of God fulfilled.

The fourth way God deals with mountains is remarkable. They do not flow down; they are not removed by God given faith; they do not become a great motorway, a highway. Instead God changes you; He gives you hind's feet (see Habakkuk 3:19). Hind's feet are delicate feet. They are not elephant's feet; some believers try to climb up the mountains God leaves in their lives with elephant's feet. They trample all over the place, but hind's feet are especially created for the most impossible crags. Hind's feet can spring from rock to rock, never falling, because God has given them the ability to overcome and reign in a place of darkness and difficulty.

Now do you begin to understand why sometimes the Lord does not always answer our prayers to remove a thorn, or smooth away a difficulty, or miraculously solve a problem in front of us? God sees the end; He is Father. He is such a good Father that He has this problem: "Shall I immediately do what this little one is crying for Me to do day and night, or shall I leave them to suffer for a while until they learn to overcome in this problem?" That is why so often, in the love of God and because He is a Father, He leaves us with the problem, and thus we learn to overcome. Once we have overcome, we shall never be the same again. Something has happened in us. It is one thing to have a mountain removed; that is some experience! A far greater experience is to have hind's feet, and to learn how to live in the mountains and traverse them.

Remember the lesson of Daniel and the lions den! The best way to overcome is to face the lions in your life. If you have all the lions removed in a miraculous way, or killed off, every time you come to a possible lion's den in your experience, the Devil can whisper and say, "If God does not remove the lions, you are finished!" The deepest level of all is to be able to go in amongst the lions, and look them straight in the eye, and find out they are nothing but pet cats. God has shut their mouths; they cannot eat you. Then what can the Devil do? He can give you a thousand lion's dens, and you will go through all of them praising the Lord, and fulfilling the purpose of God. Satan has no ground of fear in your life anymore because you have faced the worst. You faced the possibility of being eaten by the lions; you looked them straight in the eye, and found that they could not harm you.

THY PEOPLE VOLUNTEER FREELY

God the Father said to the Son: "The Lord will send forth the rod of thy strength out of Zion: Rule thou in the midst of thy enemies. Thy people offer themselves willingly in the day of thy power." We need to mark carefully that it is the Christ Himself who is to rule in the midst of His enemies; and it is the Father who makes His enemies the footstool of His feet. However we should note carefully that almost immediately we are introduced to the people of God who voluntarily stand with Him in the day of His power.

We who belong to the Lord know very well that we live in the midst of spiritual enemies. From the moment we experienced a new birth, the powers of darkness dog and plague us. The problem we face is the co-relation between the enthroned Messiah, seated and triumphant, and the situations, the circumstances, and the conditions which we, who are physically alive, encounter in this Age and in this world. On the one hand the Lord Jesus has totally won. Satan cannot touch Him, cannot dethrone Him, and cannot frustrate the Father's purpose for Him. The end is spectacularly secured! On the other hand we have the ostensible power of Satan's host, and their apparent victory again and again when they oppose the purpose of God for the redeemed and for the nations. Consider for a moment the divisions, the factions and the heresies which have rent the Church of God throughout its history. There have been times when the powers of Evil and Darkness have virtually extinguished the light of God in the Church; when the Church has become as worldly and as corrupt as the world around it. At other times Satan has apparently extinguished the Testimony of Jesus by martyring the believers.

If it had not been for the "rod of His strength" being stretched forth and sent forth out of Zion; if it had not been for the simple but glorious fact that the Lord Jesus rules in the midst of His enemies, the work of God would have been liquidated. The Messiah, however, has ruled in spite of His enemies. Again and again He has initiated movements by the Holy Spirit from the throne of God, which have kept the light of God burning on the earth. In such movements we see the Testimony of Jesus being held in spite of opposition and often martyrdom. Faithful believers have gone to their death calmly and with faith, knowing that their Lord has won.

We who have been saved by the grace of God are joined by the Spirit to the Lord Jesus at the right hand of God. A union has been produced through the Holy Spirit, which cannot be broken. Our position "in Christ" is the work of God Himself. We need illumination to understand that in Him and by Him we are to stand. Once we learn to stand within the will and mind of God and proclaim His Lordship and His victory, we are in the train of His triumph. We have to learn how to "be strong in the Lord, and in the strength of His might;" how to "put on the whole armor of God," which is the Lord Jesus. In this great conflict we are wrestling with principalities, with powers, with world-rulers of this darkness, with hosts of wicked spirits in the heavenly places. We have to learn as the Church and as believers how we can stand within His revealed will, and withstand when there is an "Evil Day," and having done all, continue to stand. That "all" can cover a vast area of problem and circumstances, from personal matters to national matters! It is not doing "our own thing," or simply following our own will and mind. It is the discerning of His will in any matter which is vital and practical, whether international, national, local, or personal. The Spirit of God alone can reveal the Lord's mind and will to us, and He is far more willing in any situation to reveal it, than we are to hear Him.

THE ROD OF HIS STRENGTH

"The Lord will send forth the rod of thy strength …" The Hebrew word translated by the English word "rod," means a staff, a rod, or a branch which has been shaped as a symbol of authority. This was the same word that we find in Exodus 4:2: 'What is that in thy hand?' And he said, 'A rod.' And he said, 'Cast it on the ground.' This was the rod that Moses used in all His dealings with Pharaoh and then later lifted it over the Red Sea to divide it. It was the rod that God used to bring water out of the rock. It symbolized divine authority.

It is also the same word we find in Numbers 17:2-3: "Speak unto the children of Israel, and take of them rods, one for each fathers' house, of all their princes according to their fathers' houses, twelve rods: write thou every man's name upon his rod. And thou shalt write Aaron's name upon the rod of Levi; for there shall be one rod for each head of their fathers' houses." There had been a rebellion against Aaron, and the Lord had directed Moses to place these rods in the

Tabernacle before the Ark of the Covenant. The Lord then said: "The rod that buds, that will be the one who has My authority." When they came in the morning, they found Aaron's rod had not only budded; it had blossomed and fruited all on the same rod. The whole cycle of the seasons had been fulfilled from bud to fruit. What does that mean? Only when there is divine authority in our midst, when it is not only recognized but obeyed and experienced, can the will of God be fulfilled amongst us. That is why so often we can get together a little group of believers but there is very little life and very little fruit. When we recognize the Headship of the Lord Jesus Christ, learn how to bow to that Headship, and to discern His mind; to understand His will together, and to obey it, we experience abundant spiritual life and abundant spiritual fruit. It is the Headship of Christ practically experienced, through His resurrection power, by the members of His body. This is the meaning of the rod budding, blossoming, and fruiting!

"The Lord will send forth the rod of thy strength out of Zion." If we paraphrase this it might bring home more clearly what is meant: "The Lord will send forth thy divine authority out of Zion." It is important to note that it is God the Father who sends forth from Zion the divine authority of the Lord Jesus. Wherever there are redeemed ones gathered together upon that foundation of Jesus Christ, being built up together into a habitation of God in the Spirit, there He will send forth the divine authority of the enthroned Lord Jesus out of Zion.

THE BODY RULES UNDER THE HEAD

"And he put all things in subjection under his feet, and gave him to be head over all things to the Church, which is his body" (Ephesians 1:22-23a). Where is His body? It is between the head and the feet! Under the feet of the Messiah, God the Father is placing the enemies of the Lord Jesus. It is important to note that Paul by the Spirit of God writes that the Father has placed "All things in subjection under His feet." He then emphatically enforces this truth by stating that God: "Gave Him to be Head over all things to the Church, which is His body."

We are in Christ! He is Head over all things to His body, and everything has been placed under His feet. That is the divinely given position of the true Church. We are the Zion of God, the place where the Name of the Lord has been caused to dwell, His holy habitation. The truth is astounding! We are joined to the Lord Jesus who is Head over all things to us, and under whose feet all things have been placed. From this glorious position, we are to face all the enemy's intrigues, his strategies, and his devices.

LEARNING TO USE THE KEYS OF THE KINGDOM

We should understand exactly what the Lord Jesus meant when He said to the Apostle Peter: "And I also say unto thee, that thou art Peter, and upon this rock I will build My Church and the gates of Hades shall not prevail against it. I will give unto thee the keys of the kingdom of heaven: and whatsoever thou shalt bind on earth shall be bound in heaven and whatsoever thou shalt loose on earth shall be loosed in heaven" (Matthew 16:18-19).

It is essential that we understand these words of our Lord Jesus. He had already said that upon the massif of the rock, which is Himself and His finished work, He would build the Church. He then went on to speak to Peter, as representing the redeemed, the living stones out of which the Church of God would be built. The Messiah said: "I will give unto thee the keys of the kingdom of heaven." Keys represent authority; whoever has the keys has authority. It was as if the Head of the Church was saying: "I am giving this authority to one who will prove how weak he is, will fail, and who will be restored. He will then open for the first time, the door to the Samaritans, and then to the Gentiles." It is of vital importance to recognize that the authority which the Lord Jesus was investing in Peter was wholly linked to His own authority; it was delegated authority. Peter as representing all of us could not act on his own authority, but had to recognize that it was the authority of the Lord Jesus. Once again we face the fact that we need to discern what is the will and the mind of Christ, to exercise His authority.

It is very sad that the words of the Lord Jesus have been so misconstrued and abused. "Whatsoever thou shalt bind on earth shall be bound in heaven and whatsoever thou shalt loose on earth shall be loosed in heaven." The two verbs which are used here " to bind" and " to loose" should be translated "whatsoever thou shalt bind on earth, shall have been bound in heaven" and "whatsoever thou shalt loose on earth shall have been loosed in heaven." These verbs in the Greek are perfect passive participles. There is no possibility of our just pontificating on what we think should be bound and should be loosed, as if we can take authoritative action and the Lord has to support us whether it is His will or not! We can only declare and proclaim what is the sovereign will of God.

If we fail to stand up in the Name of the Lord, and declare what is the truth, we have no one to blame but ourselves when the enemy lays siege to us, blockades us, and puts us into a spiritual straightjacket, binding our ability to move freely in the Lord. The powers of darkness are always seeking to rob and to spoil those who belong to the Lord Jesus. Satan's hosts are past masters at causing spiritual rheumatism and arthritis in the assemblies of God's people. The condition deteriorates whilst nothing is done about it. It needs those who are walking with the Lord and in fellowship together to stand up in prayer times and declare that the saints are God's free men and women. This lesson is one of the most difficult to learn. Yet in essence, it is absolute simplicity! Once the eyes of the heart have been opened to see the enthroned Lamb, and we open our mouths and declare that the Lamb has won; Satan has to lift the blockade or siege. It is beyond his authority and power to blockade Christ.

The practical question is: will we accept the verdict and the will of the powers of darkness or will we trust in the finished work and purpose of our Redeemer? It is a collision between God and Satan, between Christ and the powers of darkness. Why should we put up with the enemy and with his devices? Why should we allow him to impose his will upon us? We are the liberated people of God; we have not been raised in a spiritual Egypt, we are out of Egypt! God has redeemed us, loosed us from our sins and delivered us from the power of darkness. We should rise up in the Name of the Lord and ensure that the divine authority of our risen Head is exercised in our midst! Where there is heaviness, let us rule it; where there are difficulties, let us reign over them in the Name of the Lord; where there are inroads that Satan is making, let us spiritually, in prayer, confront them. Where there is ignorance of the whole counsel of God, of the eternal purpose of God, let us stand for illumination and revelation in the knowledge of Him. Let us take our position as seated with Christ in the heavenly places.

By this we do not mean that we should talk to the Devil, and that we should be forever speaking with the powers of darkness. We must leave that to those who have divine authority vested in them.

There are individuals who run around all the time rebuking Satan. They tell me they are safe but they are not safe; in the end they will trip up and will uncover themselves. Our covering is the Lord in the Church; it is as members of the body of Christ and under His Headship that we are to act, and not individually. When the Church, in the Name of the Lord, rebukes the enemy and says, "The Lord rebuke you, Satan," Satan is rebuked by our Head. He is set back. Exercising divine authority is not an individual matter, it is a Church matter.

We have to learn how to use the keys of the kingdom of heaven, how to proclaim that Jesus is Lord. We have to learn how to declare the will of God, not merely in petition, but in faith. In other words, we have to learn to say out loud, "The Lord Jesus has won; He is triumphant in this company of believers; He is Lord over the local rulers of darkness." That is the way to confront the enemy. Do not talk to him, talk to God. When we express the truth about anything, the powers of evil have to take a step backwards. They know that it is true. The enemy steps back when you make positive statements. When you say, "O Father, we bless Thee and praise Thee. The Lord Jesus Christ has been made Head over all rule and authority and power in this city."

THE CHURCH IN ASCENDANCY

Dear people of God, shall we play at Church? Or shall we rise up and experience what it is to be the living, functioning body of our Lord Jesus? God wants us to be people of vision, who see the objective of God and have an understanding of the times in which we live; a people who are totally committed to the eternal purpose of God, and it's bearing upon our lives; who are ready to be built together, and related to one another in Him.

In the final analysis it is not a matter of playing at Churches but of walking with the Lord. When we walk with the Lord, we will have a hearing ear, and we shall be sensitive to Him. Once we begin to respond to Him, we can begin together to exercise spiritual authority and executive prayer. Whether it is personal problems or corporate problems, whether it is national or international problems, we need to discern the mind of the Lord in it all. Whatever it is that blocks the way between the Lord Jesus and the fulfillment of His purpose, we need to stand in Him and with Him, for those enemies to be defeated through His finished work. We need to enforce the will of God, and pray: "Thy kingdom come. Thy will be done as in heaven so on earth" (Matthew 6:10).

If we do not learn like Moses to lift up the "rod" in the Name of the Lord, we shall never come to the throne. It is in this life, and on this earth, that we as the Church and as believers need to learn how to reign with Christ, how to enforce and realize His full victory. All the grace and all the power is available to us. It is for you and me to appropriate those resources. Even with the highways to Zion implanted in our heart, we need still to have the "rod of His strength" with us.

Chapter 5

IN THE DAY OF THY POWER THY PEOPLE ARE FREEWILL OFFERINGS

Psalm 110:1-3—The Lord saith unto my Lord, Sit thou at my right hand,
Until I make thine enemies thy footstool.
The Lord will send forth the rod of thy strength out of Zion:
Rule thou in the midst of thine enemies.
Thy people offer themselves willingly
In the day of thy power, in the beauty of holiness:
Out of the womb of the morning
Thou hast the dew of thy youth.

See Exodus 35:4-9, 20-29—And Moses spake unto all the congregation of the children of Israel, saying, This is the thing which the Lord commanded, saying, Take ye from among you an offering unto the Lord; whosoever is of a willing heart, let him bring it, the Lord's offering: gold, and silver, and brass, and blue, and purple, and scarlet, and fine linen, and goats' hair, and rams' skins dyed red, and sealskins, and acacia wood, and oil for the light, and spices for the anointing oil, and for the sweet incense, and onyx stones, and stones to be set, for the ephod, and for the breastplate.

See I Chronicles 29:1-19—Now I have prepared with

all my might for the house of my God the gold for the things of gold, and the silver for the things of silver, and the brass for the things of brass, the iron for the things of iron, and wood for the things of wood; onyx stones, and stones to be set, stones for inlaid work, and of divers colors, and all manner of precious stones, and marble stones in abundance. Moreover also, because I have set my affection on the house of my God, seeing that I have a treasure of mine own of gold and silver, I give it unto the house of my God, over and above all that I have prepared for the holy house ... I know also, my God, that thou triest the heart, and hast pleasure in uprightness. As for me, in the uprightness of my heart I have willingly offered all these things: and now have I seen with joy thy people, that are present here, offer willingly unto thee.

Shall we pray:

Oh Father, we want very simply to bow before Thee to recognize our absolute dependence upon Thee if we are to hear Thy word, if it is to be spoken, and if we are really to hear it with the ears of our spirit. Oh Father, we want to thank Thee for the anointing which is ours in the Lord Jesus Christ. We stand together into that anointing for speaker and for hearer. Make this a meeting with Thyself, Lord. Make it, we pray, a time when our hearts are stirred by Thy Spirit, challenged by Thy Spirit, where we are brought face to face with the real issues in this whole matter to do with Thy purpose concerning our Lord Jesus and concerning Thine own. Oh Father, we give this little time to Thee. Would Thou use my weakness, the dust that I am, somehow or other, to reveal Thyself and speak Thy word. And grant, oh Lord, since we are all but dust, redeemed by Thy grace, that we shall know Thy speaking and working in our midst in the most wonderful way. And we ask it in the name of our Lord Jesus. Amen.

IN THE DAY OF THY POWER

There is a significant connection between the first two verses of Psalm 110 and the following verse. The change, in one sense, is so dramatic that one is tempted to wonder whether some verses, which would have naturally led us into the truth contained in verse 3, have fallen out of the text. Since the Holy Spirit is the author of the Bible, He has also watched over the transmission of its text. Psalm 110 is exactly as God intended it to be.

The Psalm begins with an unequivocal and dogmatic statement. God the Father said to the Son: "Sit thou at my right hand, until I make thine enemies thy footstool." From the various quotations of this statement in the New Testament, we understand that it is referring to the Messiah Jesus. In simple language, we are told that Jesus has sat down at the right hand of God, awaiting the work of the Father to make His enemies His footstool. It is abundantly clear that the Lamb, the Lion of Judah, has won! The work of our salvation has been completed without the need for anything to be added to it. That finished work of the Lamb has become the ground, not only for the salvation of all those who put their trust in Him, but of also their Christian life—their service, their transformation, and of the building up and completion of the Church. It is also the ground alone upon which God's Eternal

Purpose stands.

The second statement is as unambiguous as the first. God the Father declares that "He will send forth the rod of thy strength out of Zion: Rule thou in the midst of thine enemies." It is a clear reference to the sovereign authority and power, which the Father has committed into the hands of the Son. It could not be more obvious! It is not referring to the exercise of His authority and power in Heaven amongst those who belong to God but His rule amongst and over His "enemies."

Suddenly, dramatically, His redeemed people appear! "Thy people offer themselves willingly in the day of thy power, in the beauty of holiness" (Psalm 110:3 mg). It is not the vast concourse of the redeemed of which He speaks, but of a certain remnant of the redeemed who are described as those who "offer themselves willingly" (ASV), or "volunteer freely" (NASB), or "shall be volunteers" (NKJV). Is there a connection between this group and the enthroned Messiah and the work of the Father?

It is in the day of His power that all of this takes place. The Hebrew word "Hayil," translated by the English word power means "strength" or "power" or "wealth" or "army." The ascension and glorification of the Lord Jesus was certainly the day of His power, of His wealth, and of His army. Mark carefully Revelation chapters four and five. These are exactly the words that the innumerable angelic hosts use, as they worship the enthroned Lamb: "Worthy is the Lamb that hath been slain, to receive the power, and riches, and wisdom, and might, and honor, and glory, and blessing." This is followed by the words of every created thing in the universe: "Unto Him that sitteth on the throne, and unto the Lamb, be the blessing, and the honor, and the glory, and the dominion, for ever and ever" (see Revelation 5:12, 13).

It seems reasonably clear that there is a living connection between these first fruits of the redeemed, and the enthroned Messiah, and the work of the Father. It is on this matter that there has been more than a little confusion, excess, and error, to which attention has already been drawn. Some take the truth so far that they believe in the Christianization of the whole world, including its political, educational, and social systems. On the other hand, there are many who do not even possess and experience what the Lord has so dearly won for them. This has produced a kind of passivity in the Church and in the believer; the idea is held that only in the hereafter will we know the triumph of the Lord and its consequences. It is true that some of the major consequences of His victory are in the future, but believers are meant in this earthly life to: "Lay hold on that for which also I was laid hold on by Christ Jesus" (Philippians 3:12). Both these extremes lead to problem and error.

THY PEOPLE ARE FREEWILL OFFERINGS

It is apparent from reading a number of the translations of this Psalm, that some of its verses have presented problems to the translators. They have wrestled with obscurities in the original Hebrew, especially in verse three. For example in the Jerusalem Bible and in the New English Bible, they have rendered the AV: "Beauty of holiness" as "mountains of holiness." Another problem to which we have already drawn attention is the widely differing translations of the Hebrew word "nedabot." It is rendered in this verse by a variety of English words: "volunteers," "voluntariness," "freenesses," "willing," or "willingly" etc. etc.

In the New American Standard Bible, which is probably the best rendering of this verse, it is translated: "Thy people will volunteer freely in the day of thy power." The Hebrew "nedabot" is of tremendous interest because it is a word which is used throughout the Old Testament for "freewill offering." Those freewill offerings are described in Exodus 35 and 1 Chronicles 29. A literal, although awkward translation would be: "Thy people are freewill offerings in the day of thy power, in the beauties of holiness." Carefully note that it does not state "thy people give or make freewill offerings" but "thy people are freewill offerings." That is an enormous difference!

What are freewill offerings? The burnt offering, the sin offering, the trespass offering, the peace offering, and many of the other offerings were required by the Law of God given through Moses. You could not approach God or be in a relationship with God, unless you offered those offerings. A freewill offering, however, was something that you gave of your own volition, above and beyond what was required of you by the Law. If one wants to be saved, one has to know

Christ as the burnt offering, the sin offering, the trespass offering, the peace offering, and the meal offering of God. That may not be clear to one, but if it was restated one would begin to understand. The only way a human being can be saved is to know Christ as the once-for-all and acceptable offering to God. He has won your salvation by the offering of Himself. The moment you stand upon the foundation of Jesus Christ and Him crucified, however sinful and depraved you are, however bound in evil habits and sinful ways, or however unworthy you are, God accepts you because: "Him who knew no sin He made to be sin on our behalf; that we might become the righteousness of God in Him" (II Corinthians 5:21). If we would go on to know the fullness of our salvation, the fullness of His life, and the fullness of His power for service, then we have to come alone on the basis of Christ's finished work. That is the one necessity. If however you want to see the city of God built, and built together, as God's eternal center of government; if we want to be part of the Bride, of the wife of the Lamb, we have to be a freewill offering.

The Tabernacle—every part of it—was built out of the freewill offerings of the people of God. They could never have touched the Lord but for the Passover Lamb. It was the Passover Lamb that had won them and redeemed them to God; by His blood He had loosed them from their sins. It was His power that took them through the Red Sea as on dry ground with their enemies destroyed. However, if they wanted God to dwell among them, if they desired the habitation of God, then all the materials for the construction of both the Tabernacle and the Temple were to be freewill offerings.

THE HOUSE OF GOD BUILT WITH FREEWILL OFFERINGS

In Exodus 35 you discover that everything in the Tabernacle came out of these freewill offerings. Where came the gold for the Great Lampstand, the seven-branched menorah, or the gold for the Shewbread Table, or the gold for the Golden Altar of Incense, or all the gold for the Ark of the Covenant? All that gold, and the gold which overlaid the planks of the floor and the walls came from bracelets, signet rings, earrings, and nose rings which the people took off and freely gave. From where came the silver for the things of silver? Likewise it came from the armbands, ankle bands, necklaces, and earrings of silver which were freewill offerings. Where did the wood come from? It came from the Sinai Mountains, and the acacia trees; from those who had cut the wood down and then freely given it. From where came the purple and scarlet and blue and fine white linen? It came as freewill offerings. Where did the precious stones come from that were set in the high priest's breast plate and on his shoulders? From where came the bronze for the Altar of Burnt offering, or for the Laver? They all came from the gifts which the people of God made. The whole house of God was built out of the freewill offerings of God's people.

It is remarkable, and cannot be coincidence, that when the Temple was built some four hundred or so years later by Solomon, the exact same thing happened. It was the freewill offerings of David, of his captains and leaders, and of the people of God, out of which the Temple was built.

Here is a most precious truth that what we received freely from God, we received through the finished work of our Lord Jesus Christ, but what He receives from us is the house of God. We win all His salvation—that is our inheritance; He wins us—that is His inheritance. He wins us as His Bride, as His Wife, as His Zion, as the New Jerusalem.

Those offerings were compulsory through which the children of Israel alone could approach God and come into His presence, and hear Him and be heard of Him. For the house of God to be built, however, it had to be through freewill offerings. You could still be saved and not make a freewill offering; not give even a single bangle, earring, or anything else! You could hold on to everything that was yours and still enjoy salvation; you could be in a relationship with the living God and be part of His covenant people, but have nothing whatever to do with the building of the House of God. It was those alone whose spirits stirred them up to give freely and totally to the Lord, who were building the House of the Lord. Indeed it is true that to be built together, we have to be freewill offerings. In this matter of becoming His habitation, of knowing His authority and life, and the exercise of that divine authority in the Name of our Lord Jesus the Messiah, we have to be freewill offerings.

"Thy people are freewill offerings in the day of thy power, in the beauties of holiness." In the day of Your power, Your people are freewill offerings. They give themselves freely without thought for their own pleasure or self satisfaction. It is not that they give freewill offerings, even at great cost, they are themselves freewill offerings. Out of such devotion to the Lord, out of a basic self denial, and the surrender of their human rights, the House of the Lord is built. Such believers have become the bondslaves of the Lord Jesus! There is a very great difference between a hired servant and a bondslave. A hired servant has certain working hours; he has pay and rights, etc. The bondslave was owned twenty-four hours of each day and week and year!

IN THE BEAUTIES OF HOLINESS

We should mark carefully that those who are described as freewill offerings in the day of His power are also described as being clothed with the "beauties of holiness." We should note that the Hebrew is in the plural. It should never be forgotten that when the High Priest, or the priests, went into the Presence of the Lord, they were especially clothed (see Exodus 28). They could not appear before the Lord, or be involved in any divine service, without those garments. It was not left to them as to how to clothe themselves. There were garments of righteousness, and also garments of beauty and majesty. It is the basic idea which the translators sought to convey with their rendering of the Hebrew in the English Revised version, the American Standard Version, and a number of other modern versions: "In holy array." However, unless you know your Bible very well, those words tend to have little meaning and seem awkward and artificial!

In fact it has tremendous meaning and significance. We can never appear before the Lord in the garments of our own righteousnesses, but only clothed in the righteousness and holiness of the Lord Jesus. Nothing less than that is acceptable to God. Furthermore, those who are described as "Freewill Offerings," the most devoted and mature of the redeemed, are also to be clothed in the "beauties of holiness," in the garments particularly ordered by God. Whoever we may be amongst the redeemed of the Lord, we need to be clothed every time we appear before the Lord in the garment of the righteousness of the Messiah and in the garment of the majesties and beauties of His character.

Within no other righteousness can a saved fallen human being stand in the Presence of the Lord, whether he is a newly saved sinner or a great apostle, also saved by the grace of God.

FROM THE WOMB OF THE DAWN THY YOUTH ARE TO THEE AS THE DEW

We have the same problem with this statement as with the rest of verse 3; there are many differing translations. The Hebrew is ambiguous and allows these different translations. It can be translated: "From the womb of the morning, thou hast the dew of thy youth." Thus some Bible teachers have felt that it is a reference to the Lord Jesus and the New Day that dawned with His birth. The translation of the NASB, "from the womb of the dawn, thy youth are to thee as the dew," is not only a possible translation of the Hebrew, but it is in keeping with the spiritual sense of the Psalm. It refers to those who are freewill offerings in the day of His power.

Those who are born of God and devoted to Him, who are prepared to go the whole way with Him, have recognized and understood the real significance of the birth of the Lord Jesus. They have understood that it was a new creation that came with Him at His birth. It was a new age, a new day, a new man that had dawned with His coming, and it will end in a New Jerusalem coming down out of heaven having the glory of God, and a new heaven and a new earth wherein dwells righteousness.

Such believers who, by the power of the Holy Spirit and the grace of God, are prepared to follow Him fully whatever the cost, who have become living sacrifices are to the Lord Jesus truly like "a glass of cold water in the desert." Those born of the Spirit through the work of the Lord Jesus are born into this New Creation, into this New Day and into this New Man. They are perennially youthful through the exceeding greatness of the power of His resurrection. Like the dew, they become a joy and a refreshing to the Lord Jesus.

Dew is an extraordinary phenomenon! It is silent, for no one has ever heard it fall! Quietly it comes and refreshes the tired, hot, weary ground. In Israel you suddenly discover that your car looks as though it has rained, but it has not rained; it never rains in the five month dry season. It is the dew! In ancient times before irrigation all the fruits such as peaches, nectarines, grapes, dates, and pomegranates ripened with the dew. It is a picture of the continuous and quiet work of the Holy Spirit keeping us alive and fruitful. The redeemed, who are freewill offerings in the day of His power, are by the Spirit of life in Christ Jesus experiencing the quiet, regular refreshing of the Lord. They in turn become refreshment to the Lord Jesus. They have a ministry to Him which is unique. As born again believers we hear all the time about the ministry of Christ to the Church, to believers, and to the unsaved world, but we rarely hear of ministry to the Lord. This is a ministry which means everything to the Lord Jesus.

There was, you will remember, a certain woman who came to the Lord Jesus with an alabaster cruse of expensive pure liquid nard, broke it and anointed His head. Often people, who could afford it, had bought such an alabaster cruse of aromatic spice in ointment or liquid form to be saved and used at their death. The disciples were scandalized by the waste of money that her act cost, protesting that it could have been sold and the money used for the poor. Jesus however, said: "Let her alone; why trouble ye her? she hath wrought a good work on me ... She hath done what she could; she hath anointed my body beforehand for the burying" (Mark 14:6, 8).

It was a ministry to Him which none of the other disciples had performed. So significant and precious was this woman's act to Jesus that He said: "Wheresoever the gospel shall be preached throughout the whole world, that also which this woman hath done shall be spoken of for a memorial of her" (Mark 14:9). Those who are freewill offerings are such people! They love the Lord so much, that in ministering to Him, they spare no expense. The Lord Jesus had said something over this act of hers that is rarely mentioned, or even noticed. He linked it to the Gospel, as if she had come to the heart of the matter. She lavished on Him the most costly item that she had, because she had understood that He was on His way to His death. How much she saw, we do not know; it was probably a good deal more than we think she understood. This act of sacrificial love meant much to the Lord Jesus. Those who are freewill offerings to the Lord are those who have understood something of the wider meaning of His death, burial and resurrection. For them the Gospel has not only led to conversion and discipleship; it has led them to be wholly spent and lavished on Him. Such disciples become as dew to Him!

It is a fact worth recording that the Gospel of John is not so much a history of the Lord Jesus, as a remarkable interpretation of His life and work; and that Gospel ends with the risen Lord asking the leader of the coming Church: "Simon, son of John, lovest thou Me more than these? Then He said: "Feed my lambs" (John 21:15). A ministry to the Lord Jesus is the highest and most essential calling of a child of God, or of a servant of the Lord. Out of that love and ministry to Him comes the feeding of the lambs and the tending of the sheep.

This is why the Lord Jesus was prepared to move the lampstand away from the Church in Ephesus, probably the most remarkable Church of the seven Churches to which He spoke. They were so hard working, discerning, well taught, patient and enduring, and with great understanding. They lacked in only one matter: "Thou didst leave thy first love. Remember therefore whence thou art fallen, and repent and do the first works; or else I come to thee, and will move thy lampstand out of its place, except thou repent" (Revelation 2:4-5 mg).

These instances of the risen Lord speaking to His own make us aware of the simple fact that ministry to Him, which flows out of a self-sacrificing love, means more to Him than we can ever describe.

THE LOVERS OF THE LORD JESUS

Those who have become freewill offerings in the day of His power are not a naturally superior people. They are not elitist, who arrogate to themselves far more authority and power than they should. For them "the Lamb is all the glory in Immanuel's Land." Simply, they are those who are possessing and appropriating what has been won for them in their "so great salvation." The enthroned Lamb is for them the Alpha and the Omega of God's language. He is the first and the last, the beginning and the end, and the Amen of God. Those who are freewill offerings in the day of His power are simply and supremely lovers of the Lord Jesus.

Chapter 6

THE POWER OF HIS RESURRECTION

Psalm 110:1-3—The Lord saith unto my Lord, Sit thou at my right hand,
Until I make thine enemies the stool of thy feet.
The Lord will send forth the rod of thy strength out of Zion:
Rule thou in the midst of thine enemies.
Thy people are freewill-offerings
In the day of thy power,
In the beauty of holiness:
Out of the womb of the morning
Thy youth are to thee as dew.

A word of prayer:

Oh Father, as we come once again to this Psalm, we want to confess and recognize again before Thee that without Thee we can do nothing. Whether in speaking or hearing, Lord, apart from Thee there will be nothing of eternal value, nothing that will go through into the building of Zion unless, Lord, Thou art present and Thou art the enabling power and grace of speaker and hearer alike. Lord, how glad we are that Thou has not left us to our own resources, but Thou has made provision for us and the anointing which is upon our Head, the Lord Jesus. We thank Thee that that anointing includes every redeemed one, and we thank Thee for the portion of the anointing for both speaker and hearer alike. Into that we stand by faith. Would Thou make this time together a meeting with Thyself in Thy Word. Would Thou take Thy Word and write it indelibly upon our hearts? Would Thou release something of Thyself, Lord, so that in our lives Thy Word becomes flesh and blood? Oh Father, hear us, as together we commit this time to Thee in the name of our Lord Jesus. Amen.

OUT OF THE WOMB OF THE DAWN

Those who are born of God are saved not only by the finished work of the Lord Jesus, but also by His resurrection life. The Apostle Paul writes: "For if while we were enemies, we were reconciled to God through the death of His Son, much more, being reconciled, shall we be saved by His life" (Romans 5:10). If the finished work of the Lord Jesus is the legal ground upon which God gives us everything, the power of His resurrection life becomes the practical capability and means by which we experience all that He has given us through that finished work. When we were born of the Spirit, we were born into a New Creation, into a New Day. That New Creation came with the birth of the Lord Jesus; and that New Day dawned with His birth. We only become part of that New Creation, and enter that New Day, by the death of the Lord Jesus for us, and by a new birth through His resurrection from the dead by: "the exceeding greatness of His power to us-ward who believe" (see Ephesians 1:19-20). All the power of Satan and his host were mobilised to keep Christ in the grave but they all failed. That eternal life, which overcame the power of death, is in us who believe.

In the exceeding greatness of His resurrection

power, there is everything which the Church or the believer could need. In the Messiah Jesus we have a life that died, was buried, was placed in a tomb and broke out of it in triumph. It is no wonder that the Apostle Paul writes in his testimony: "That I may know Him, and the power of His resurrection, and the fellowship of His sufferings" (Philippians 3:10). To know the Lord in a real and genuine manner requires that we know the power of His resurrection; it requires also that we enter the fellowship of His sufferings. All the power we need to experience that which He has won in His death for us is within that resurrection life.

"Out of the womb of the dawn, thy youth are to thee as dew." When we as the living Church or as true believers, recognize the significance of the coming of the Lord Jesus, and keep within that new beginning, we are as dew to Him. The Messiah called Himself the Alpha and the Omega; He is the alphabet of God (see Revelation 22:13). To know the heart and mind of God, we have to learn that new alphabet. The Lord Jesus is the Word of God. The Greek logos translated by the English Word means "a thought that is concretely expressed." When a person does not speak or write, we have no idea as to what is in their heart or mind. Their thought is hidden; it is unrevealed. When we use words, we express what is in our heart and in our mind so that others can understand. The Lord Jesus is the alphabet of God; He articulates the thoughts of God. When we hear Him, when we see Him, we understand the heart and the mind of God. We do not need to have the philosophy or the wisdom of this world to understand the living God; we need Jesus! The problem is that demonic forces are at all times seeking to infiltrate the world's ideas, its standards, its fashions, and its philosophies into the life of the Church and into the life of the believer. This is the most powerful and continuous battle which the people of God face. When the Devil and his minions are permitted to work in that manner, it always ends in death and corruption.

The enthroned Messiah also calls Himself "the first and the last, and the beginning and the end." In other words, He is everything. He is the first and the last and all that is in-between; He is the beginning and the end and all the development between the start and the finish. It is interesting to note that in Revelation 1:17 He says: "Fear not; I am the first and the last, and the Living one." Everything we need of power, of ability, and of energy, is within His life. We have no reason to fear. All these titles of the Lord Jesus convey the same idea—that He is everything. With Christ has come a New Creation, a New Day, and a New Man.

In Christ a New Day has begun, with a new order, a new power and a new destiny. The old day is heading for final judgment and destruction, the New Day for Divine glory. We, who are born again of the Spirit of God, have been called "out of the womb of the dawn."

A NEW CREATION

The Apostle Paul writes: "Wherefore if any man is in Christ, there is a new creation: The old things are passed away; behold, they are become new. But all things are of God, who reconciled us to Himself through Christ" (II

Corinthians 5:17-18 mg).

The marginal rendering is best, for the original Greek can admit both translations. This New Creation is Christ, and by the grace of God, we are in Christ. There, the old has passed away, all things have become new. However in many of us believers, the old man, the old creation, hangs on. Once again the words of the Lord Jesus have great and significant meaning in this matter: "Abide in Me and I in you. As the branch cannot bear fruit of itself, except that it abide in the vine; so neither can ye, except ye abide in Me ... For apart from Me ye can do nothing" (see John 15:4-5). There is a New Creation in Christ. The Lord Jesus, the one who is sitting on the throne, as recorded in Revelation 21, declares: "Behold, I make all things new." It is interesting to note that this is immediately followed by: "I am the Alpha and the Omega, the beginning and the end." All the newness is in Him and of Him.

It is quite apparent to all who are born of God that we are not in the New Creation but in the old. We see, hear, and experience everything which belongs to a fallen and old creation. We, however, are in Christ and there is the New Creation. If we abide in Him, and He in us, we are kept within that New Creation. It is the enemy's strategy to get us out of the covering which is ours in Christ. No matter how prevalent is the darkness, or how much the enemy works within the world system, or how seemingly powerful is Satan, it makes no difference; there will come a day when all things will be made new. The New Creation will come into its fullness. It is perfectly clear if we read the Word of God carefully, that the natural creation, whether feather, fur, or fin, is included in this final New Creation (see Romans 8:18-25). In that New Creation Christ will be all in all.

The true and living Church is born into this New Day, and into this New Creation. We are the first fruits, and also the heralds of its final coming and triumph.

THE NEW MAN

The New Man was born with the birth of the Lord Jesus. He is the Second Man, the New Man; Adam was the first. He is the Last Adam, who in Himself has concluded the whole sad saga of the first Adam, the fallen man, including all of us before we were saved. This New Man is being: "Renewed unto knowledge after the image of Him that created him: where there cannot be Greek or Jew, circumcision and uncircumcision, barbarian, Scythian, bondman, freeman: but Christ is all, and in all" (Colossians 3:10-11). Note carefully this New Man is being "renewed unto knowledge after the image of Him that created him."

There is a process in a genuine believer walking obediently with the Lord, whereby he is being transformed and changed into the image of the One who created him. Note also that in this New Man, there is none of the racial or ethnic divisions, or the religious or social divisions which are natural to the old man; and belong to that old order.

This is confirmed when Paul writes: "Wherefore remember, that once ye, the Gentiles in the flesh, who are called Uncircumcision by that which is called Circumcision, in the flesh, made by hands; that ye were at that time separate from Christ, alienated from the commonwealth of Israel, and strangers from the covenants of the promise, having no hope and without God in the world. But now in Christ Jesus ye that were once far off are made nigh in the blood of Christ. For He is our peace, who made both one, and brake down the middle wall of partition" (Ephesians 2:11-14).

We should notice that we are told by the Spirit of God to "put on" the New Man and "put off" the old man (see Colossians 3:9-10). The very words used, and the manner in which the action is described, requires a positive action on the part of the child of God. One does not drift into it. Unfortunately we become so used to Biblical language that its meaning does not always come home to us. There is a whole list of sinful and bad habits which belong to the old man and which we are told to put away. Likewise we are told to: "Put ye on the Lord Jesus Christ, and make not provision for the flesh, to fulfil the lusts thereof" (Romans 13:14).

It is here that we begin to realize how important is the "exceeding greatness of His power to us-ward who believe;" for left to ourselves we become passive. We become Christian drifters, like bodiless phantoms occupying seats in the meeting, drifting in and drifting out. When His power energises us, we not only: "Fight the good fight of the faith;" but we are enabled to "lay hold on the life eternal to which you were called" (1 Timothy 6:12 NASB). Within that eternal life of the Messiah is all the power that we shall ever need.

THE POWER OF HIS RESURRECTION

In the testimony of Paul contained in his Philippian letter, he speaks of: "Knowing the power of His resurrection." We need to realize that he was not writing about academic knowledge but of practical experience. There is a world of difference in knowing the doctrine, recognizing the truth as the truth, and experiencing personally the power of His resurrection in ones own circumstances and life.

Our problem, yours and mine, is that we may have been born of God, but we rarely experience the power of His risen life. To know and experience practically the power of His resurrection transforms our lives. We are energized by Him to face in a new manner the opposition, the enemies, the problems, and the satanically inspired circumstances; by His grace we then overcome them all.

Life has incredible power! I have often held in my hand the seeds of a pine tree—little, dried up, shrivelled, brown looking seeds. There seems to be no life in them whatsoever. If that little seed, however, falls into a crevice of a great boulder in the mountains, what happens to it? When the rain fall reaches it, and the sunlight touches it, it germinates. That silly, little seed, shrivelled and dried up, germinates; and its little roots go down and somehow a strange small main shoot grows out of it. If one could talk to it, one would say "You silly little thing, why did you choose of all places a crevice in this massive rock? You must be mad! Do you think that you are going to live?" That little seed would look at us, and if it could see itself, it would probably die of shame! One would say to it, "Look at you, down at the bottom of that huge rock with your funny little white whiskers on your bottom, and a little tiny straggly shoot on your top: You have chosen suicide! What do you think you are going to do with this great boulder which weighs so many tons? Do you not think you have made a colossal mistake?" The little seed is quiet for a moment and then says, "I have life in me which always comes out on top; always triumphs; the boulder does not. I am obeying the law of my life; I have a life in me which has exceedingly great power in it. It is true that I am small, my stature is tiny, and I look so silly and weak. Compared with me the boulder is enormous. Weigh me; you would not even have to use a feather as a weight in the balances. Weigh the boulder; it weighs tons. But I have a life in me and there is a law in that life, and I am obeying the law of that life, and so I grow."

Go back in a few years time, and you will see something remarkable. The whole boulder is split open, and a tree has grown up. How did it happen? It happened because that little seed obeyed the law of its life. There was power in that life to overcome its problems, to overcome all the difficulties, and everything that was against it. That little sapling finally split the rock wide open. If you have been in the mountains of Europe or America or Asia or Israel, or anywhere in the world, you will see many illustrations of such boulders, which have been split open by a tree that began as a little, tiny, shrivelled up seed. So is the power of His resurrection in a saved human life. If that child of God obeys the law of its life, he or she will overcome.

Many of us have circumstances and problems which are as impossible as that great boulder. It seems that nothing could humanly overcome those difficulties. At times it seems as if the very light is shut out. If, however, we learn to trust and obey the "law of the Spirit of life in Christ Jesus," there is not a single problem which the life of Jesus cannot overcome. Eternal life is eternal life! The Lord Jesus repeatedly declared that He is that life. "I am the way ... and the life; I am the resurrection, and the life" (see John 14:6, 11:25). This eternal life has been given to us as a free gift, based on the finished work of the Messiah. That life is the Lord Jesus! John writing in his first letter stated: "And the witness is this, that God gave unto us eternal life, and this life is in His Son. He that hath the Son, hath the life; he that hath not the Son of God hath not the life" (1 John 5:11-12). No amount of religious ceremony or ritual, whether it be with water in many different forms of baptism; or in bread and wine in countless forms of communion; or in the right hand of fellowship, which places one's name on a membership roll, can ever substitute for a genuine Holy Spirit conversion and new birth. When we are born from above through the work of the Spirit, we receive that eternal life.

The life which the Lord Jesus brought to us, eternal life, came with Him at His birth in Bethlehem, and went through all the difficulties and problems of childhood, of youth, and adulthood in Nazareth. That life in the Messiah, in the three years of His Messianic ministry suffered every form of contradiction, of opposition and of gainsaying, and triumphed. It went through Gethsemane; it was for Jesus the great crisis of the will of God for Him, and He triumphed. That life in the Messiah went through the mockery, the scourging, the bruising, and reached the goal, Calvary. At Calvary the Prince of life was crucified, and the work of our salvation was completed. He was laid in a tomb, but it was impossible for death to hold that life; it burst forth from the tomb victorious. It was Jesus who was that life, and who gives us that life, who ascended to the right hand of God, and obtained the promise of the Spirit for us and poured Him forth. If we are born of God by the Holy Spirit, that life, which has an incredible history, is in us. It has overcome more than any of us will ever face. If we will only learn to trust and obey the Spirit of life which is in us, we also will overcome. It is an overcoming life. The Messiah Himself has said it: "These things have I spoken unto you, that in Me ye may have peace. In the world ye have tribulation: but be of good cheer; I have overcome the world" (John 16:33). Note carefully that He did not put the emphasis on us. He could have said: "Be of good cheer, ye shall overcome the world." What He did say was: "Be of good cheer, I have overcome the world." In other words, He in us will be the overcomer.

When I was still a boy and my sister was a little girl, we would come home from school together, and we always used to pass through the parish graveyard. There were great stones in that graveyard, engraved with the names of people who had been buried for hundreds of years. Sometimes we would see the vicar. Since neither of us ever went to a Church or synagogue, he represented Christianity for us. He was dressed in a black gown reaching to the ground, and he was a frightening figure to us, because he had never been known to smile. He had a face like death, and we used to think that he had risen from a grave in the parish church-yard with not too much life in him. He sort of drifted like a spirit, or a ghost, through the place. We used to hide from him because we were so afraid of him.

However, there was in that graveyard a great family mausoleum, a family tomb, and at some time the seed of a silver birch tree had fallen into that tomb. One cannot think of anything more unlikely or less conducive to that seed germinating and growing than in a large family tomb! The Church building, the graveyard, the vicar, and the family tomb all spoke of death. There should not have been much dampness in that vault, but somehow or other the seed of that most beautiful and fragile tree, found everywhere in Northern spheres of Europe, had fallen into that family mausoleum and germinated. How it lived I do not know, but it had obeyed the law of its life, and it grew and grew. It came out of a crack on the side of the family tomb, and slowly it had grown up into a graceful tree, into the sunshine of the heavens. It lifted the whole top of the family tomb and split it. Some years ago the Church authorities decided to clear the graveyard and make it a more pleasant place for people to sit in. They cleared away the family tomb, but they left the tree. Now there is a beautiful tree standing in a place of death, a symbol of life, of power over death, and the circumstances which should have destroyed it are gone.

Some of us are in circumstances like that family grave. Everything is against us, but if once the seed of God's life gets into that situation, and we obey the law of its life, then it can do no other but grow up into the heavens. It will grow up towards the light and warmth of God, until in the end it breaks open the very thing that should have destroyed it. There will come a day, when those circumstances have passed away, but the tree will be forever. It is a tree of the Lord's planting.

If only we understood a little more about the power of the resurrection of Jesus. "Out of the womb of the dawn, thy youth are as dew to thee." The Lord has made a provision for us that we might be refreshment to Him. When we come in the beauties of holiness; in the garments of salvation and the garments of praise, knowing and experiencing the power of His life, and finding our all in Him, we become a joy to the Lord and perennial refreshment to Him. Our growth in Him, our transformation become a ministry to Him, something of great preciousness to Him. He then sees the fruit of His travail and is satisfied. We have become as refreshing dew to Him!

THE LAW OF THE SPIRIT OF LIFE IN CHRIST JESUS

"For the law of the Spirit of life in Christ Jesus made me free from the law of sin and of death (Romans 8:2).

Have you ever tried to deal with the law of sin and of death? Everyone knows what it is like. You cannot love some person. It is the law of sin and death. You have jealousy in your heart, you have intense rivalry, you have covetousness, you are highly opinionated to the point of being factious. All of these things and many more that we could mention are symptoms of the law of sin and death. When we try to deal with it, it is like a large aircushion; no matter where we push it down it will always come up somewhere else! What can we do with the law of sin and death? The more you try to deal with it, the more dominant it becomes. The more one tries to stop coveting, the more covetous one becomes. Those who have tried to live the Christian life ought to have had much experience along this line. The more one tries to live the Christian life, the more impossible it becomes to live that life. It is an exhausting experience in continuous failing.

The Apostle Paul wrote: "The kingdom of God is not eating and drinking, but righteousness and peace and joy in the Holy Spirit. For he that herein serveth Christ is well pleasing to God, and approved of men" (Romans 14:17-18).

For those who seek to please God and to live this Christian life, these words seem to be a mockery. I write from experience; for some four years I did my utmost to be a good Christian. I did not find the righteousness, the joy and the peace, of which the Apostle speaks; instead my life was a pressurized tension! I did my best to be a good Christian; I learnt the Christian phraseology and used it; I put aside a little time each day to read the Word and to pray; and I adopted John Wesley's plan of speaking to at least one person each day about their soul's salvation. However my life was a misery, it was all law and little grace. I used to look at all those shining faces singing Charles Wesley's great hymn:

> Long my imprisoned spirit lay,
>   Fast bound in sin and natures night
> Thine eye diffused a quickening ray,
>   I woke, the dungeon flamed with light;
> My chains fell off, my heart was free,
>   I rose, went forth, and followed thee.

However, my chains had not fallen off and my heart was not free! I was truly saved and born of God, but my Christian life consisted basically of not doing certain things and of doing other things. Many years later, I discovered that nearly all of those shining faces had the same experience as myself. I even discovered that the preacher, who was always preaching about victory, did not experience that victory himself, but preached it "in faith." Decades later, he told me himself.

The work of the ministry which God has given me, takes me all over the world, and the question that young people ask me most often is: "How can I live the Christian life?" I answer always in the same manner. The question is not "How can I live the Christian life?" but "How can I die?" If a child of God knows how to give up all right to himself or herself, and take up the cross and follow Him; if he or she learns how to fall into the ground and die, the "living" of the Christian life takes care of itself. It is similar to natural law; it is cause and effect. If you know how to die, the Holy Spirit takes care of the "living." This is: "the law of the Spirit of life in Christ Jesus."

The Apostle Paul put this simply in stating: "I have been crucified with Christ; and it is no longer I that live, but Christ liveth in me: and that life which I now live in the flesh I live in faith, the faith which is in the Son of God, who loved me, and gave Himself up for me" (Galatians 2:20). Carefully note that this is all about living. "Christ liveth in me ... that life which I now live ... I live in faith." The key to this life is to recognize that one has been crucified with Christ.

If a child of God knows how to fall into the ground and die, the Lord can place him or her anywhere, and in that place there will be abundant fruit. It is cause and effect! Resurrection life is never mentioned in the New Testament without being coupled with the death of the cross. How can we know the "exceeding greatness of His power" unless we accept "the sentence of death within ourselves, that we should not trust in ourselves, but in God who raiseth the dead: who delivered us out of so great a death, and will deliver" (II Corinthians 1:9-10). We are not only to "know Him, and the power of His resurrection ..." but also "the fellowship of His sufferings" (see Philippians 3:10).

We only know the power of His resurrection through the death of our Lord Jesus. Through His death, and through it alone, we are not only saved and born of God, but we experience His risen life. In His life is all the practical energy and power which we need. However, apart from our being prepared to lose our self-life, there is no way we can know His resurrection life in full power and reality; it remains a doctrine. There is no alternative to the death of the cross if we are to experience the power of His life!

Sometimes I have sat on a jumbo jet and watched the four hundred people piling into that massive aircraft. I have looked down from the windows, as high as my second floor bedroom window, and thought to myself, what an enormous plane, with four hundred passengers and a crew of 35! I have looked at the four engines; in each of which I could stand up fully. Then I have wondered how this huge aircraft is going to take off with all its weight? I have looked at the sizes of some of the people, some of whom are three times the normal size; I have watched all the food being loaded onto the plane; and I have seen the passengers' luggage being stored in its holds. Then I have thought that this aircraft will never get off the ground! I remembered from school days one of the few scientific lessons that remained in my head; it was the law of gravity. I know from my own experience, that if I go up to the balcony and step over the railing, I shall fall. It is cause and effect. How is this enormous plane with four hundred and thirty five people on board, with all the luggage and food, going to get off the ground? Then we taxi down to the runway and turn onto it. Without even slowing down it takes off from it, majestically and with ease! It did not fight with the law of gravity; another more powerful and superior law overcame it. That giant plane with all those people on board soared into the heavens into the sunshine far above the clouds.

When the Spirit of life in Christ Jesus dwells in us, unhindered and unlimited; when we have given Him all the keys to all the rooms in our life; when He is allowed to be Lord and allowed to be free to work as He desires in our life, then the law of the Spirit of life in Christ Jesus makes us free from the law of sin and death. A superior and more powerful law has overcome the lesser law.

HE WILL DRINK OF THE BROOK BY THE WAY

"He will drink of the brook in the way: Therefore will He lift up the head" (Psalm 110:7). Here at the end of this Psalm we have again the same thought; it is the renewing, reviving, and energizing life of the risen Christ. It is the power of His resurrection. The Lord Jesus by the Spirit drank of the brook of His Father's life all the way from Bethlehem to Calvary. At no single point did He not draw from the life of His Father. He said many times: "I do nothing of Myself, but as the Father taught Me I speak these things" (John 8:28).

Again: "The Son can do nothing of Himself, but what He seeth the Father doing" (John 5:19).

Or again: "For I spake not from Myself; but the Father that sent Me, He hath given Me commandment what I should say, and what I should speak" (John 12:49). The Lord Jesus was drinking of the brook in the way that was His Father's will for Him. It was a way that was foreordained by God.

All the way He had to walk, the brook was there. He drank of that brook through all those years when He was a carpenter and stonemason; through those three years of His Messianic ministry with all its conflict, its difficulties and its gainsaying. He drank of that brook in Gethsemane. It was very hard for Him, but in the end He drank from it and said: "Father not as I will but as thou wilt." He drank of it on the cross, for the writer of the Hebrew letter declared: "Who through the eternal Spirit offered Himself without blemish unto God" (Hebrews 9:13). He drank of the brook all the way that was the will of God for Him until He reached the throne of God.

This word translated by the English word brook in Hebrew is "Nahal." Those who have visited Israel will know this word by the popularly used Arabic word Wadi. It is a seasonal mountain torrent. When the former or latter rains have fallen, over many years great gorges have been carved out by these torrents in the mountains and wildernesses of Israel. Even in the hot dry season, there is this brook in the bed of the wadi buried under meters of rock and soil.

"He will drink of the brook in the way." It is important to note that in the Hebrew there is an emphasis. It is not "any" way, but the way. In other words, it is the will of God; the only way the master went. We disciples will have to go the same way which the Lord travelled. If we are going to traverse the highways to Zion, there is no alternative. That way is not some broad, flat, highway, a motorway upon which you can travel with comfort and speed. The way of the Lord will often be winding and tortuous; that way goes up in the mountains, and passes through difficult terrain. Wherever the will of God takes you, wherever the highway to Zion leads you, there is always the brook in the way. Do not faint, or give up! Find the brook, for it is there. It may not always be apparent, but it is there. As you drink from it, you will lift up your head in the way.

It is said of the Lord Jesus that He drank of the brook in the way, and that as a result He lifted up the head. The word "lift up the head" means that the head is exalted, or lifted up. That is how the Lord Jesus came through; He drank of the Spirit. Putting it in New Testament terms: He made sure that nothing came out of Himself but everything was out of the Father.

This has also a tremendous lesson for us. The only way we will ever traverse this highway to Zion is when we do everything out of Christ. It has always to be of Him. All our beginnings and our sources are to be in Him. Satan's strategy has always been the same. It is to deceive us into believing that some of our springs should be from other sources than the Lord Jesus. That is the point where humanism or the world's philosophy or wisdom is sown into our thinking with dire and deadly consequences. It is the same with the power of His resurrection. There is a power that is of the flesh, which is psychically produced. It can appear to be genuine spiritual power, but it is not; many are deceived by it. There is, however, real power and it comes through the resurrection of Jesus. It is that power which the Holy Spirit makes a reality to us and in us.

THE EXCEEDING GREATNESS OF HIS POWER

One can have all the equipment and all the gadgets, from cookers, dishwashers, washing machines, dryers, hot water kettles, computers, and telephones, but if there is no electrical power, they are useless. The house can be filled with everything that one could possibly need, but without the power, it is all practically ineffective. Of course one still has all the equipment and the different gadgets, but they simply "look pretty."

This is like many assemblies and communities of believers when the power of God is not present; it is precisely the same with an individual believer's life. Through the finished work of the Lord Jesus, God gives us everything in our salvation. Without the power of His resurrection there is little effect. We are saved, we are born of God, but there is nothing put into action. This can be the same with a fellowship of believers: We have the doctrine, the truth, the Gospel, but there is no power. We preach and hear great truths, but there is no practical effect.

There is no alternative to the person and work of the Holy Spirit! He alone makes the resurrection power of the Lord Jesus a living reality to us. Without Him we are divorced from practical reality.

One of the aspects of the work of the Holy Spirit is that He continuously refreshes and renews the servants of God, the believers, and the assemblies of His people. It is the "brook in the way." When we drink of that brook, our head is lifted up. We have to learn the simple but practical lesson: we need to drink and drink again.

Chapter 7

CHRIST AS PRIEST AND KING

Psalm 110:4-6—The Lord hath sworn and will not repent:
Thou art a priest forever after the order of Melchizedek.
The Lord at thy right hand
Will strike through kings in the day of his wrath.
He will judge among the nations,
He will fill the places with dead bodies;
He will strike through the head in many countries.

Psalm 110 is a small Psalm of seven verses, and therefore might not appear to be significant or important. In fact with God littleness and brevity does not mean irrelevance. Take for example the common saying: "Can any good thing come out of Nazareth?"
Or, "But thou, Bethlehem Ephratah, which art little to be among the thousands of Judah, out of thee shall one come forth unto Me that is to be ruler in Israel; whose goings forth are from of old, from everlasting" (Micah 5:2). It was the Messianic King who was to be born in Bethlehem, and to live in Nazareth for at least some twenty years.
Zechariah also reminds us: "For who hath despised

the day of small things?" (Zechariah 4:10)

And again Isaiah says: "The little one shall become a thousand, and the small one a strong nation" (Isaiah 60:22). With God littleness is by no means the measure of importance or significance!

In the fourth verse of this Psalm we come to another much quoted and extremely important matter: "The Lord hath sworn, and will not repent: Thou art a priest forever after the order of Melchizedek." We should note carefully the dogmatic manner in which the Holy Spirit introduces the Messianic Kingship and High Priesthood of the Lord Jesus. He declares solemnly that the "Lord hath sworn, and will not repent." This alone should capture our attention! The Lord is introducing a matter of the utmost importance. In fact, we could say that the whole Bible hinges on the Messianic Kingship and the High Priesthood of the Messiah. In the New Testament the Messiah's Kingship is everywhere emphasised, and His High Priesthood underlined.

THE PROMISE OF A MESSIANIC KING

When John had that amazing vision of the little Lamb as slaughtered in the midst of the throne, the Elder introduced the Lord Jesus as: "The Lion that is of the tribe of Judah, the Root of David" (Revelation 5:5). In the last vision which John saw, Jesus said: "I am the Root and the offspring of David, the bright, the morning star" (Revelation 22:16). In those two sentences, not only Jewish history is encompassed, but Divine history; the whole of the Bible is covered.

The Messianic King had been promised from the

beginning of time. When man fell the Lord had predicted: "I will put enmity between thee and the woman, and between thy seed and her seed: he shall bruise thy head, and thou shalt bruise his heel" (Genesis 3:15).

It was the Divine promise of a Messiah to be born of a woman. Much later the Lord declared through Jacob that the Messiah would be born of the tribe of Judah: "The sceptre shall not depart from Judah, nor the ruler's staff from between his feet, until Shiloh come; And unto him shall the obedience of the peoples be" (Genesis 49:10). As he was dying King David prophesied by the Spirit: "The Rock of Israel spake to me: One that ruleth over men righteously, that ruleth in the fear of God, he shall be as the light of the morning, when the sun riseth, a morning without clouds ...Verily my house is not so with God; Yet He hath made with me an everlasting covenant, ordered in all things and sure: For it is all my salvation" (II Samuel 23:3-5). The Messianic King was destined to be born of the royal line of King David.

We have in the New Testament, both the pedigree of Jesus through Solomon and His pedigree through Nathan. It has been suggested that one was the royal line through Joseph, and the other the royal line through Mary. What is abundantly clear is that Jesus was born of royal stock. It is often said that Jesus was a peasant, but in fact He had only royal blood in His veins. It is an interesting fact that Jesus wore a robe that belonged to the noble or higher class; it was woven without seam and very valuable. For this reason at Calvary the soldiers cast lots as to who should have the robe.

Even the Talmud says of Jesus, calling Him "Yesu," that He was born of royal stock. Unfortunately the great building which housed all the archives and pedigrees was destroyed in the Roman siege and destruction of Jerusalem from 66-70 AD, with the loss of all the pedigrees. It is a fact that everywhere Jesus went He was hailed as "Son of David;" it was as if people were hailing Him as the crown Prince of the House of David. Even when He died, Pilate wrote the inscription which was nailed above His head, "This is Jesus, the King of the Jews;" and when the Chief Priests, and some others tried to persuade Him to change the wording, He would not, with the famous words, "What I have written, I have written." Peter preaching his famous message on the day of Pentecost concluded it with these words: "Let all the house of Israel therefore know assuredly, that God hath made Him both Lord and Christ, this Jesus whom ye crucified" (Acts 2:36). Note the words Lord and Christ; it means "King" and "Messiah." God confirmed the Messianic Kingship of Jesus by His resurrection from the dead and His ascension to the right hand of God.

THE WORTHINESS OF THE KING

Through history there have been many evil kings, who have been savage, brutal, and tyrannical. There have also been many good and godly kings. Those who live in a Republic tend to think of all kingship as evil; it is almost impossible for such to believe that there could be a king who served his people selflessly and sacrificially. Yet the character of true Kingship is sacrificial and selfless service. Jesus was—throughout His life on earth—innately good. Although tempted on all points, He was without sin, and remained so. What he preached, He practiced. He was the royal bondslave of God, always serving. Tirelessly and patiently He endured the gainsaying and contradiction of sinners. Even when crucified and in agony, bearing at the same time the taunts of the Chief Priests and Scribes, He made provision for His mother's well-being and future. In the humiliation and ill treatment of the Lord Jesus at the hands of the High Priest and Chief Priests, and the coarse Roman soldiers, we see in Jesus the kind of character that is worthy to reign as king.

He had already been tried before the Sanhedrin where many had spat on His face, had buffeted Him, and hit Him. Then the cohort in the praetorium took Him, stripped Him of His clothing, and put a scarlet robe on Him. They platted a crown of thorns and rammed it on His head, and placing a reed in His right hand they knelt before Him, mocking Him saying: "Hail, King of the Jews."

At such a point, when divested of all authority, of even your normal clothing, and cruelly mocked, human beings usually lose all sense of dignity; He remained with the character of a king. He never responded with curses or oaths; he never lost His temper but maintained His dignity. There has never been a crown more powerful than that crown of thorns, nor a sceptre more authoritative than that reed. At that point, the angelic host in Heaven must have been prostrate on their faces in worship. It is no wonder that when the whole of creation worshipped Him after His passion and ascension, they said: "Unto Him that sitteth on the throne, and unto the Lamb, be the blessing, and the honor, and the glory, and the dominion, for ever and ever" (Revelation 5:13).

Jesus has not only the pedigree of the royal Davidic line; in character He is utterly worthy to be King forever. He has shown and proved in His life on earth the kind of character that can do no other than come to the throne. It is interesting to note that the refrain throughout all the worship in the book of Revelation is about "the worthiness of the Lamb." They sing, "Worthy art thou ..." or "Worthy is the Lamb ..."

A PRIEST FOREVER AFTER THE ORDER OF MELCHIZEDEK

The statement of Divine intent "thou art a priest forever after the order of Melchizedek," is quoted a number of times in the New Testament. It draws our attention to the fact that the Messiah is prophesied to be both King and High Priest.

There was in the Old Testament a strict law that a High Priest could not act as King, and a King could not act as High Priest. It was stipulated that the two orders be kept totally separate from one another. It was King Uzziah who sought to combine in himself the two offices. He took a censer, filled it with incense, and went to the Golden Altar to offer it to the Lord God. The High Priest Azariah and eighty other priests had confronted him and rebuked him. He had lost his temper and immediately had been struck with leprosy. He remained a leper until his death, segregated from all normal life (see II Chronicles 26:16-21). This incident ensured that no other king would try to combine the two offices into one.

The amazing prophecy in this Psalm was that the Messiah, who was to come, would be both King and High Priest. There had been in the whole long history of the people of God under the Old Covenant, apart from King Uzziah, only one case of a person who combined within himself the two offices. His name was Melchizedek (see Genesis 14:17-24). He is also called King of Salem, which means King of Peace. Salem was almost certainly the original name of Jerusalem and thus Melchizedek was King of Jerusalem. The meaning of Melchizedek in Hebrew is King of Righteousness. The very fact that Melchizedek could bless Abram, speaks volumes. It was not a few empty, religious words, but a genuine blessing of God which came upon Abram; it was meaningful.

It is interesting to note that it was predicted by the Holy Spirit through David that the Messiah would be a Priest "after the order of Melchizedek." It simply meant that the Messiah would combine within Himself the two offices of King and High Priest. The writer of the Hebrew letter states that the Lord Jesus: "Became unto all them that obey Him the author of eternal salvation; named of God a High Priest after the order of Melchizedek" (Hebrews 5:9-10). Again He states: "A hope both sure and stedfast and entering into that which is within the veil; whither as a forerunner Jesus entered for us, having become a high priest forever after the order of

Melchizedek" (Hebrews 6:19-20).

It is absolutely clear from the seventh chapter of the Hebrew letter that Jesus is our High Priest. That chapter concludes with the words: "For it was fitting that we should have such a high priest, holy, innocent, undefiled, separated from sinners and exalted above the heavens; who does not need daily, like those high priests, to offer up sacrifices, first for His own sins, and then for the sins of the people, because this He did once for all when He offered up Himself. For the Law appoints men as high priests who are weak, but the word of the oath, which came after the Law appoints a Son, made perfect forever. Now the main point in what has been said is this: we have such a high priest, who has taken His seat at the right hand of the throne of the Majesty in the heavens, a minister in the sanctuary, and in the true tabernacle, which the Lord pitched, not man" (Hebrews 7:26-8:2 NASB). Note carefully that this "word of the oath which came after the Law" is a direct reference to Psalm 110:4. The Lord gave that "word of the oath" concerning the promised Messiah through King David many centuries after He gave the Law through Moses.

WE HAVE SUCH A HIGH PRIEST

The point of all this is that we have an eternal High Priest enthroned at the right hand of God, who ever lives to make intercession for us. Will we ever know how much we owe to His intercession, whether as the true and living Church, or whether as His servants in the work of the Gospel, or whether as individual believers, in our families, in our business life or workplace? We are told: "Christ entered not into a holy place made with hands, like in pattern to the true; but into heaven itself, now to appear before the face of God for us" (Hebrews 9:24).

Or again: "Wherefore also He is able to save to the uttermost them that draw near unto God through Him, seeing He ever liveth to make intercession for them" (Hebrews 7:25).

It is interesting to note that when the Lord Jesus spoke of the Holy Spirit being given as an "advocate," He said: "I will pray the Father, and He shall give you another Advocate" (John 14:16).

The Apostle John also used this same word when he said: "If any man sin, we have an Advocate with the Father, Jesus Christ the righteous" (1 John 2:1). The word in Greek is Parakletos and it means an "intercessor," "a consoler," or "an advocate;" someone who pleads the cause of anyone before a judge. The Lord Jesus is such an advocate and intercessor who appears before the face of God for us so that we may be kept from the Evil One and kept in His Name.

The High Priestly prayer of the Lord Jesus, as it is recorded in John chapter 17, is a window into the heart of the Lord Jesus as our intercessor and advocate. There, before His passion, the agony of the cross, He prayed for those whom the Father had given Him.

"I pray for them: I pray not for the world, but for those whom Thou hast given me; for they are Thine ... Holy Father, keep them in Thy Name which Thou hast given Me, that they may be one, even as We are. While

I was with them, I kept them in Thy Name which Thou hast given Me: and I guarded them, and not one of them perished, but the son of perdition; that the Scripture might be fulfilled ... I pray not that Thou shouldest take them from the world, but that thou shouldest keep them from the evil one ... Neither for these only do I pray, but for them also that believe on Me through their word; that they may all be one ... Father, I desire that they also whom Thou hast given Me be with Me where I am, that they may behold My glory, which Thou hast given Me" (John 17:9, 11, 12, 15, 20, 24).

This moving prayer of the Lord Jesus as our High Priest gives us some clue to His advocacy and intercession for us. Note carefully: "I pray ... for those whom thou hast given Me." "Keep them, in Thy Name which Thou hast given Me, that they may be one." "Keep them from the evil on ... I desire that they also whom thou hast given Me be with Me where I am." It was not only for the eleven disciples that He interceded, but for all of us who have believed on His Name: "Neither for these only do I pray, but for them also that believe on Me through their word."

HIS INTERCESSION FOR THE BUILDING AND COMPLETION OF THE CHURCH

The Messiah Jesus made a dogmatic declaration when He said: "Upon this rock I will build My Church; and the gates of hell shall not prevail against it." These words of the Lord Jesus furnish us with an understanding of much of His intercession for the Church, which the Father has given Him. There has been a continuous and colossal conflict on this earth, a war waged by Satan, to frustrate the Messiah's building of the Church. If we look at the Church, we note an ebb and a flow throughout its history. The building of it has been challenged at all times. If it had not been for the intercession of the Lord Jesus, the building of the Church would have altogether stopped, and it would have degenerated into a worldly institution and organization. However, the Lord Jesus in intercession has taken the initiative, and new movements of the Spirit of God have been launched many times, and the building work of the Church has progressed. There are many names associated with these movements, such as the Donatists, the Montanists, the Paulicians, the Bogomils, the Albegenses, the Waldenses, the Priscillianists, the Reformation, the Puritans, the Covenantors, the Quakers, the Anabaptists, the Mennonites, the Stundists, the Moravians, the Methodists or Enthusiasts, the Brethren, the Pentecostals, and the Charismatics. This is only to mention some of those names: The Lord Himself alone knows the full story.

There are many names also associated with the successful intercession of our Lord Jesus, to mention but a few—John Wycliffe, John Huss, Martin Luther, Ulrich Zwingli, George Fox, John Knox, Hugh Latimer, Thomas Cranmer, Nicholas Ridley, Count Zinzendorf, John Wesley, George Whitfield, J N Darby, George Muller, Robert Cleaver Chapman, Anthony Norris Groves, Theodore Austin-Sparks, Watchman Nee, Brother Bakht Singh, and so one could go on!

Without the continuous advocacy and intercession

of the Lord Jesus there would be no story to tell. If the torch of the Testimony of Jesus is still held today, it is wholly due to the intercession of our High Priest. The story has not ended yet! The true and living Church of God is now moving into one of the most difficult and dark periods of world history. It will survive and triumph, not through its own ingenuity, but through the intercession of the Lord Jesus; the time for the Top stone finally to be fitted will come!

HIS INTERCESSION FOR THE WORK OF THE GOSPEL

The risen Lord Jesus, shortly before His ascension and glorification, met His disciples and said: "All authority hath been given unto Me in heaven and on earth." Then He commissioned them: "Go ye therefore, and make disciples of all the nations baptizing them into the Name of the Father and of the Son and of the Holy Spirit: teaching them to observe all things whatsoever I commanded you: and lo, I am with you always, even unto the end of the world" (Matthew 28:18-20).

We should note that the statement of the Lord Jesus that all authority in heaven and on earth had been given into His hands, is not to be left as doctrinal truth, important as that may be. He immediately followed that stunning statement with the commission: "Go ye therefore." Mark the little word therefore, for it links His present position and power with His commission "to go." Further note that a tremendous promise is made to those who obey: "And lo I am with you all the days, even unto the consummation of the age" (mg). It is a tremendous promise! All His power and authority, His gifts and equipment and everything else we need in the work of the Gospel, will be ours. Most marvellous of all, by the Holy Spirit He Himself will go with those who obey this commission until the work is completed.

The history of the work of the Gospel is a chequered one, much the same as the history of the building of the Church. If the Gospel has reached the ends of the earth and been preached in almost all nations, it is due completely to the intercessory work of the Messiah and those who have obeyed His commission. That is not to state that the Lord's commission is totally fulfilled at this present point in time; there are still areas of this world where the Gospel has not been preached as a testimony.

In the early years of the Church, the work of the Gospel spread like wildfire. Within a matter of decades it had reached Ethiopia in the South; Egypt, Libya and Tunisia in North Africa; Greece, Italy, Serbia, Croatia, Bosnia, Romania, Bulgaria, Germany, France, Spain and Great Britain, in Europe; it had reached Armenia in the North and Southern India in Asia. For this progress to be achieved many lives had been laid down in devotion to the Lord Jesus.

Apart, however, from truly bright patches, the work of the Gospel then slowed down considerably. The whole enormous thrust forward came with Christians like William Carey who felt called to take the Gospel to India. There can be no doubt that this was due to the intercession of the Lord Jesus. In Matthew's Gospel the Lord Jesus had spoken about His coming again when He said: "And this Gospel of the kingdom shall be preached in the whole world for a testimony unto all the nations; and then shall the end come" (Matthew 24:14). This sense of the Lord's soon return, and the fact that the work of the Gospel had not yet been completed, became the driving force for this great move forward.

There are many servants of God, who pioneered this work of the Gospel, whose names have become known throughout the believing Christian world. It has truly been the intercession of the Lord Jesus which has produced these servants of God, who have left all and gone into strange and foreign surroundings to preach the Gospel. His intercession has kept them in His Name, and kept them from the Evil One, and enabled them finally to reach His throne. The Lord Jesus has kept His promise to be with them all the days, even unto the end of the age; and however much more work has to be done, His promise still stands.

HIS INTERCESSION FOR THE BELIEVER

From the throne, at God's right hand, Jesus intercedes for those whom He saves. A wonderful quality of the Lord Jesus is His faithfulness and loyalty to them. "Being confident of this very thing, that He who began a good work in you will perfect it until the day of Jesus Christ" (Philippians 1:6). The Lord Jesus has begun a good work in every one who is born of the Spirit, and He watches over those lives that He might bring them to maturity and full growth for the Day of His return.

Jude, in concluding his letter, says: "Now unto Him who is able to guard you from stumbling, and to set you before the presence of His glory without blemish in exceeding joy" (Jude 24). As the Lord Jesus watched over His disciples in the days of His earthly life, so now, at the right hand of God, He watches over us to guard us from stumbling, in order to set us before the presence of His glory without blemish in exceeding joy.

We should also note that "He is able to save to the uttermost ... seeing He ever lives to make intercession for us." There is no bound or limit to the ability and the power of the Lord Jesus to transform the human life He saves. The problem is more to do with us; we do not always give Him the freedom to work in our lives in the way that He desires. If we are freewill offerings in this Day of His power, He will keep us from the Evil One; and He will keep us in His Name. That is another way of stating that He will watch over us to keep us abiding in Him; for whilst we abide in Him, we will be in the center of God's will, in the safest and most secure place in this fallen and evil world.

We can learn a great amount about the intercession of the Lord Jesus for us from the manner in which He prayed for the Apostle Peter. It is a window into the character of His ongoing intercession for us. Jesus said: "Simon, Simon, behold, Satan obtained you by asking, that he might sift you as wheat: but I made supplication for thee, that thy faith fail not; and do thou, when once thou hast turned again, establish thy brethren. And He said unto Him, Lord, with thee I am ready to go both to prison and to death. And He said, I tell thee, Peter, the cock shall not crow this day, until thou shalt thrice deny that thou knowest Me" (Luke 22:31-34 mg).

This "window" teaches us a number of exceedingly important lessons. Firstly the Lord Jesus knows everything about us that there is to know. He knows our weaknesses, our failings, and our strong and good points. He never misjudges a person! In His intercession for Peter, He knew that Peter was going to fail, and fail miserably; and that it was due to Peter's blind and high esteem of himself. Simon Peter had no idea of his capacity to fall! Satan however knew that capacity, and asked for Peter, that he might try him. The Lord Jesus was fully aware of how this would affect Peter. It is worth repetition that He is never taken by surprise over those who belong to Him; He knows exactly what it would take to deliver us from the chaff in our lives, and preserve the wheat.

Secondly, Satan obtained Peter by request! Simon Peter's Christian life was "second hand;" his was a self-manufactured Christianity. It is interesting to note that Satan cannot touch a true believer, without permission from God! Peter could never have become the chief Apostle, who by the will of God opened the door first to the Jews, then to the Samaritans, and finally to the Gentiles, unless his self-manufactured Christian life was blown away.

The Lord Jesus said: "I have prayed for you, that your faith fail not." Most of us would have described what happened that night to Simon Peter as the total collapse of his faith. He did not deny the Lord once, but three times, and with oaths! The Lord Jesus knew that deeper than Peter's self-produced Christian life, there was a grain of God given faith. It took only one glance of the

Lord, when the eyes of Jesus and Peter met, for that "grain of faith" to spring into action, and Peter wept his way back to the Messiah. Satan wanted to sift Peter as wheat; he received the chaff and God received the wheat. It was due alone to the intercession of the Lord Jesus.

The Apostle Peter later wrote about this in his first letter: "Wherein ye greatly rejoice, though now for a little while, if need be, ye have been put to grief in manifold trials, that the proof of your faith, being more precious than gold that perisheth though it is proved by fire, may be found unto praise and glory and honor at the revelation of Jesus Christ" (1 Peter 1:6-7). Note that it is the "proving" or "proof" of your faith being more precious than gold that perisheth. The New King James translates it: "The genuineness of your faith." God never tries your faith, if there is no real God given faith to begin with! He only reveals what is real and genuine, that it may be strengthened.

Thirdly, it is comforting and strengthening to recognize the sensitivity of the Lord Jesus as Intercessor. Even though Peter's self-produced Christianity was blown away that night, it resulted in tremendous spiritual character. It is interesting to note that when Jesus interceded for Simon Peter, He said: "I prayed for you that your faith fail not and do thou, when once thou hast turned again, establish thy brethren." The intercession of the Messiah Jesus was positive, not negative! He interceded for Peter that his faith fail not, and then spoke words of great encouragement, that the end of that trial would be fruitful. We see how positive is the intercession of Jesus when He said: "Establish thy brethren." It was a commission given before Peter even fell! Of course, he had absolutely no idea that within hours he would fail deeply and miserably. It reveals how self-deceived we can become. He protested: "Lord, with thee I am ready to go both to prison and to death." So strong was his self-life that he believed it. Jesus knew what was in him and that he would go through this trial and lose the chaff. The intercession of the enthroned Messiah Jesus is always positive when it comes to those who are truly saved. Even when His children have to go through a valley of the shadow of death, He knows the reason for them to have to walk through such a valley; then His staff and His rod comforts them.

It has to be of enormous comfort to us that Jesus "ever lives to make intercession for us." The beginning of that verse states: "He is able to save to the uttermost those that draw near unto God through Him." We should note that we need at all times to draw near to God through Him, if we would experience being saved to the uttermost. We shall never know until we are with Him, how much the redeemed owe to His continuous and patient intercession. Everyone who fights the good fight of faith, who runs the race and wins, who finishes the course, who is found within the will of God at the end of their earthly life, owes it to the intercession of the enthroned Lamb. How can we fall short with such an intercessor, and with such intercession?

CHRIST AS KING

As we have already written, the promise of a

Messianic King is found everywhere in the Word of God. It is summed up in the remarkable prophecy in Isaiah. "For unto us a child is born, unto us a Son is given; and the government shall be upon His shoulder: and His Name shall be called Wonderful, Counsellor, Mighty God, Everlasting Father, Prince of Peace. Of the increase of His government and of peace there shall be no end, upon the throne of David and upon his kingdom, to establish it, and to uphold it with justice and with righteousness from henceforth even for ever" (Isaiah 9:6-7).

And again in Isaiah: "Behold, a king shall reign in righteousness, and princes shall rule in justice. And a man shall be as a hiding place from the wind, and a covert from the tempest, as streams of water in a dry place, as the shade of a great rock in a weary land" (Isaiah 32:1-2). And again in Jeremiah: "Behold, the days come, saith the Lord, that I will raise unto David a righteous Branch, and he shall reign as king and deal wisely, and shall execute justice and righteousness in the land" (Jeremiah 23:5).

And yet again in Zechariah: "Rejoice greatly, oh Daughter of Zion; shout, oh Daughter of Jerusalem: behold, thy King cometh unto thee; He is just, and having salvation; lowly, and riding upon an ass, even upon a colt the foal of an ass ... And His dominion shall be from sea to sea, and from the River to the ends of the earth" (Zechariah 9:9-10).

This coming King is described as absolutely righteous in all His ways; He is just and will establish and uphold the throne and kingdom with justice; He will deal wisely. His kingdom is eternal, and of it there will be no end. Moreover, of even greater personal significance, in Him will be salvation. In that salvation He will be as a hiding place from the wind, as a covert from the tempest, as streams of water in a dry land, and as a shade of a great rock in a weary land. Incredibly, He is described as "lowly;" He will not ride on a magnificent white horse, but on an ass. Of whom can this speak other than the Messiah, the Lord Jesus? He fits perfectly the picture described in these prophecies.

It is interesting to note that in Psalm 110 the moment the Messiah is introduced with a Divine oath as "Priest forever after the Order of Melchizedek," the next verses speak only of judgment. We need to be very careful in the manner in which we handle this subject. One aspect of the Messiah's Kingship and reign is His saving grace and faithfulness. To those who are born of God, He will be everything they need. The greatest lesson we can learn is to surrender our will to Him, and lay down our self-life. Upon this revolves so much! If we would grow in the Lord, if we would serve Him, if we would overcome all that is set against us, and if we would be part of His eternal building program, we must know practically in our experience His absolute Lordship. There is no alternative! For those who have surrendered to His absolute Lordship, He takes full responsibility. They are the freewill offerings in the Day of His power!

"The Lord will send forth the rod of thy strength out of Zion." The enthroned Lamb always deals with the living Church and with the true believer righteously and justly. He uses the sceptre of His strength to protect us, to provide for us, and to lead us to walk in His will.

When He deals with empires, with superpowers, with nations, or with ideologies, it is also always righteously and justly; it is with justice. Into the hands of our Lord Jesus the Messiah, the Father has committed all judgment—the judgment of empires, of nations, and of individuals.

In Isaiah it is prophesied of the Messiah: "Then a shoot will spring from the stem of Jesse, and a branch from his roots will bear fruit. And the Spirit of the Lord will rest on Him, the spirit of wisdom and understanding, the spirit of counsel and strength, the spirit of knowledge and the fear of the Lord. And He will delight in the fear of the Lord, and He will not judge by what His eyes see, nor make a decision by what His ears hear; but with righteousness He will judge the poor, and decide with fairness for the afflicted of the earth; and He will strike the earth with the rod of His mouth, and with the breath of His lips He will slay the wicked. Also righteousness will be the belt about His loins, and faithfulness the belt about His waist" (Isaiah 11:1-5 NASB).

With much of modern Christianity the judgment of the world, its leaders, and its peoples, seems to present a very large problem. Some Christian theologians and leaders have solved it to their satisfaction by relegating all judgment to the Old Testament. Apparently in the Old Testament God was a very angry being; in the New Testament He is all love and mercy! However this is no solution to the problem. Apart from the many

Scriptures which refer to final judgment throughout the twenty-seven books and letters of the New Testament, many of them spoken by the Lord Jesus Himself or by His Apostles, the last book, the book of Revelation, is full of Divine judgement, as well as of Divine salvation. There is no escape from this "problem."

Furthermore, it speaks of the wrath of the Lamb: "And the kings of the earth and the great men and the commanders and the rich and the strong and every slave and free man, hid themselves in the caves and among the rocks of the mountains; and they said to the mountains and to the rocks, "Fall on us and hide us from the presence of Him who sits on the throne, and from the wrath of the Lamb; for the great day of their wrath has come; and who is able to stand?" (Revelation 6:15-17 NASB) One does not normally associate a lamb with wrath! The book of Revelation describes the coming judgments of God in great detail; nothing is spared.

Even in some so called Evangelical circles, the judgment of sin and evil, or Hell, or even tribulation and affliction in the Christian experience is never mentioned. It is as if the Christian will never experience problem or suffering or pain; all is "peace and joy." It is, however, peace where there is no peace, and joy where there is no joy. We do not solve a theological problem by "recasting" the Word of God to say something it never said; or by simply ignoring whole portions of the Word of God; or explaining them away for the sake of the fashion of our day and generation.

In fact, there can be no righteous or just government, without the judgment of sin, of evil, and of corruption. If in the ages to come the Almighty could brush over genocide, or massacres, or murder, or rape, or fraudulence and corruption perpetrated in many cases by those who died wealthy and in peace, then it brings into question His righteousness, His holiness and His justice. God is not sentimental, whose sense of justice can be swayed. God is the God of love, of mercy, and of grace, but not at the expense of His righteousness, of His holiness, and of His justice. The only way to be saved from the wrath to come is to be saved through the finished work of the Lord Jesus. There is no other way!

God is the God of grace. It is that grace which demands final judgment for the victims of all evil and wickedness. The King who reigns in righteousness and justice can do no other.

As I have already written, the moment in Psalm 110 the Messiah is introduced as King and as High Priest, the following two verses speak of judgment: "The Lord at thy right hand will strike through kings in the day of His wrath. He will judge among the nations, He will fill the places with dead bodies, He will strike through the head in many countries" (Psalm 110:5-6). The English word strike is translated from a very strong word in Hebrew Mahats; it means "to smite through," "to wound severely," or "to shatter." The enemies or foes of the Lord have been shattered by the Messiah Himself, by His finished work on the cross. He will judge the nations; and they will be filled with dead bodies. The reason for the difference in translation of these verses is because the Hebrew is ambiguous; but it is clear that these verses speak of total and final judgment.

It could well be that in this Psalm the ambiguity is deliberate and allows for differing translations. For example, we could translate the Hebrew, "out of the womb of the morning, thou hast the dew of thy youth." It is a perfectly viable translation and would speak of the birth of the Lord Jesus—the New Day, New Man, and New Creation that has come through Him, and the permanent renewing that He gives. We could also translate this: "Out of the womb of the dawn, thy youth are to thee as the dew." Then it speaks with the emphasis upon those who have been born of God, who have been born into a New Day, and have been introduced to a New Creation, and are part of the New Man. Those who are total in their devotion to the Lord Jesus become as dew to Him. Both these translations are viable and that may well be the mind of the Holy Spirit.

No one who believes in the authority, inspiration, and relevance of the Bible, can avoid the simple fact that the Bible ends with the Judgment of the Great White Throne (see Revelation 20:11-15). That judgment is final and complete! It precedes the coming down of the New Jerusalem, the Wife of the Lamb. In those verses, it is recorded: "And I saw the dead, the great and the small, standing before the throne; and books were opened: And another book was open which is the book of life: And the dead were judged out of the things which were written in the books." From this verse it is clear that the final judgments are based on actual records. Everything that was wrong in history is righted;

nothing is passed over or forgotten.

In Psalm 110:5-6, is there any reference to Satan, the prince of this world, and his host, the principalities and powers, the world rulers of this darkness, who have been dispossessed by the ascension and enthronement of the Messiah? The Lord Jesus Himself said just before His death on the cross: "Now is the judgment of this world: now shall the prince of this world be cast out" (John 12:31). He referred to His passion and His ascension as a judgment on the Prince of this world. The writer of the letter to the Hebrews states: "He also Himself in like manner partook of the same; that through death He might bring to nought him that had the power of death, that is, the Devil; and might deliver all them who through fear of death were all their lifetime subject to bondage" (Hebrews 2:14-15). Note very carefully that the death of the Lord Jesus has brought to nought him who had the power of death, even the Devil. This surely means that the Lord Jesus has brought the works of the Devil to zero! There can be no other explanation. That incredible fact has to be realized and enforced by the Church.

There have been many different translations of the first part of Psalm 110 verse 6. Literally it would read in English, "He has shattered or severely wounded the head over much of the earth." Can we find in this any reference to the judgment of the Prince of this world, to his dispossession? In the earliest prophecy concerning the coming Messiah, the Lord Himself said to the serpent: "He shall bruise thy head, and thou shalt bruise his heel" (Genesis 3:15b). The Hebrew word translated "bruise" in this prophecy, is quite different to the Hebrew word used twice in verses five and six. Nevertheless, has this statement in Psalm 110:6a some relationship to the prophecy in Genesis 3:15b? We can say with absolute certainty that the Messiah has shattered Satan, dispossessing him of his power. His enthronement at the right hand of God is the guarantee that He has won! The triumph and victory of the Lord Jesus has to be proclaimed by us; for Satan and his forces continue to throw their weight around.

The Lord Jesus is described as the King of Righteousness and the King of Peace. It would be totally wrong to give the impression that His Kingship is all to do with judgment. It has more to do with pure and righteous government, with faithfulness and mercy, and with the peace which He brings to those who have been loosed from their sins in His blood. The King is the Saviour of the world; no one is turned away, however sinful, depraved, or humanly speaking lost in wickedness. Once He saves, He keeps, for with love and tenderness He watches over those whom He saves. His Kingship and His Priesthood are both exercised to save to the uttermost those whom He delivers. Their sin has been blotted out by the work of the Messiah at Calvary, and they have been declared righteous on the basis of His work.

"Thine eyes shall see the king in his beauty: they shall behold a land of far distances" (Isaiah 33:17 mg). There can be no doubt that those who have been redeemed by the Lord Jesus have seen the King in His beauty; for they have beheld the Lamb of God, who has borne away the sin of the world. If they have followed Him at the cost of their self-life, they have endured all, as the eyes of their hearts have seen the King in His beauty. For those who have become freewill offerings in the Day of His Power, they begin to see not only the King in His beauty, but through Him the land of far distances. They begin to see how vast and endless is His purpose, to which by His grace they have been restored.

We should carefully note how the Word of God concludes the revelation of God's heart and mind contained in its sixty-six books: "And there shall be no curse anymore: and the throne of God and of the Lamb shall be therein: and His bondservants shall serve Him; and they shall see His face; and His Name shall be on their forehead ... and they shall reign for ever and ever" (Revelation 22:3-5 mg). These bondslaves are totally owned by their master; they have no hours, no pay, and no rights. Every fiftieth year, under the Old Covenant, in the year of jubilee they could obtain their freedom. Their status is quite different to the hired servant who has hours, has pay, and has rights. These bondslaves of the Lord are apparently Kings and Priests, for they reign with God and the Lamb forever and ever. One does not normally associate a bondslave with kingship and priesthood, but the Lord does!

Movingly the Word of God reveals that these bondslaves of the Lord "shall serve Him, and they shall see His face, and His Name shall be on their foreheads." They will be so near to the King that they can see clearly His features. Truly they shall see literally the King in His beauty.

Chapter 8

MADE KINGS AND PRIESTS UNTO HIM

Psalm 110: 4—The Lord hath sworn, and will not repent;
Thou art a priest for ever
After the order of Melchizedek.

Revelation 1:6—And He made us to be a kingdom, to be
priests unto His God and Father; to Him be the glory and the
dominion for ever and ever. Amen.

Revelation 5:10—And madest them to be unto our God a
kingdom and priests; and they reign upon the earth.

It is of great practical consequence that through Him, who is both King and High Priest, we who are born of God are also made kings and priests. "And He made us to be a kingdom, to be priests unto His God and Father; to Him be the glory and the dominion for ever and ever. Amen" (Revelation 1:6). "And madest them to be unto our God a kingdom and priests; and they reign upon the earth" (Revelation 5:10). The Authorised Version, followed by the New King James Version, reads "kings and priests." Its basic Greek text is the Received text; whereas the modern versions from the English Revised of 1881 and onwards have used the Alexandrian text and other texts which are much earlier; that Greek text reads "kingdom and priests." The term in Greek Basileia properly means "royalty;" "the rule and the realm ruled," "the reign and the territory under that reign."

Theodore Austin-Sparks used to say the best way to understand this Greek word is to translate it by the English word "kingship." By this Mr. Sparks did not mean that we should translate this word only by "kingship," but that it gives us a fuller understanding of its meaning. God made us to be not merely a kingdom to be ruled over, or to reside within, but a kingship, and priests unto Him. The word kingship includes within its meaning the need for character, for discipline, for training, and for education. The Apostle Peter expresses this beautifully when he writes: "Ye also, as living stones, are built up a spiritual house, to be a holy priesthood, to offer up spiritual sacrifices, acceptable to God through Jesus Christ ... a royal priesthood ..."(1 Peter 2:5, 9). Note carefully Peter's words, "a royal priesthood." This combination of kingship and priesthood was prohibited under the Old Covenant, as has been already mentioned in the previous chapter.

The Lord Jesus declared: "Fear not, little flock; for it is your Father's good pleasure to give you the kingdom" (Luke 12:32). It is certainly true that it was God's good and merciful intention to give the kingdom to those whom He saves. If, however, we have understood the explanation given above, and use the word "kingship" instead of "kingdom," then our whole understanding of that which the Lord meant is broadened. He was not merely promising us territory to rule over, or a kingdom of peace and righteousness to live within, but He was emphasizing the character that is needed to reign with Him.

THY PEOPLE ARE FREEWILL OFFERINGS IN THE DAY OF THY POWER

We should observe that Psalm 110 begins with the declaration: "The Lord saith unto my Lord, Sit thou at my right hand until I make thine enemies thy footstool. The Lord will send forth the rod of thy strength out of Zion: Rule thou in the midst of thy enemies" (vv. 1-2). It is a dogmatic declaration of Divine intent. Twice it is stated that the Father is speaking to the Son; the first time "sit thou at my right hand until ...," and the second, He will "send forth the rod of thy strength." In verse 4 we have a further declaration: "The Lord hath sworn, and will not repent: Thou art a priest forever after the Order of Melchizedek."

The solemn manner in which the Father introduces this further statement causes us to pause, and take in that which He is stating. It is interesting to note that a number of times the writer of the Hebrew letter emphasizes this Divine Oath which was made. This is followed in verses 5 and 6, by the Son's final judgments. Sandwiched between the first two verses and the last four verses, is the statement: "Thy people are freewill offerings in the day of thy power, in the beauties of holiness: out of the womb of the morning ..." It is obvious that the enthroned Messiah is now in the Day of His Power; He is seated, and rules in the midst of His enemies. What then is the significance and the practical meaning of His people being freewill offerings? Is it not that they are to function as kings and priests under His authority?

THOSE WHO EXECUTE THE WILL OF THE LORD ON THIS EARTH

It seems reasonably clear as one meditates on this Psalm that those people described as freewill offerings are to be practically involved in His Kingship. Under the authority of the King, they are to execute His will on this earth. Note that in the pattern prayer in which the Lord taught us to pray: "Thy Kingdom come, Thy will be done, as in heaven so on earth;" the words are not mere wishful thinking, a hope that in the end His Kingdom will come and that His will should be done on earth as in heaven. It is a declaration that His Kingdom should even now spiritually, before its final and public manifestation, have influence and bearing upon our present earthly situations and problems. We are meant to bring the authority of the enthroned Lamb to bear upon the situations, the obstacles, and the problems which confront us on this fallen earth; whatever they are. The promises of God are to be stood on and realized, in both the personal sense as well as the corporate. The Holy Spirit takes the Word of God, whether in statements or in promises, and applies them to us; and when, by faith, we stand on those statements and promises, something happens. The Apostle Paul declares: "For how many soever be the promises of God, in Him is the yea: wherefore also through Him is the Amen, unto the glory of God through us" (II Corinthians 1:20). Note carefully that there is in Christ a "yes" concerning the promises of God and through Him a process until the "Amen." In other words, the promises of God are not just ideals, but the means by which we experience and know more fully the Lord. It is as the Apostle Peter wrote in his second letter: "Whereby He hath granted unto us His precious and exceeding great promises; that through these ye may become partakers of the divine nature" (II Peter 1:4a).

AUNTIE ELLA AND HER SEWING MACHINE

It was Auntie Ella who first introduced me to the practical nature of the promises of God, and that once applied by the Holy Spirit to our situation or problem, we had to stand on them by faith. It was in the Church in which I came to know the Lord that I also came to know this old sister. Many in the Church thought that she was eccentric; in fact some thought that she was nuts! She had lived her whole life in the cultural world; she had been an opera singer with her husband. Then she had come to know the Lord. I knew her as Auntie Ella. From her salvation and onwards, she had a real and ongoing experience of His power and grace. She was always talking about the Lord as if He lived with her, whereas most Church members only talked of the Lord when the pastor came to tea! She used to say: "When I go home to the Lord and I have seen Him, and talked with Him, I shall make a bee line for Isaiah, because I have a number of questions to ask him." With her the Bible lived. I remember her saying on another occasion: "O, that young man Zephaniah, how I love him." I had no idea that Zephaniah was a young man; I knew nothing about him and what he had prophesied.

My sister had a contralto voice, and Auntie Ella was training it. I used to go and collect my sister after her lesson. This occasion was to change my life by changing my attitude to the Word of God. When I arrived at Auntie Ella's apartment, I discovered that my sister had already gone home with a friend. Auntie Ella said: "Dear boy, come in and have a cup of tea." So I went in. She apologized for the fact that her living room was not tidy; she had her sewing machine out and lots of material, and was obviously busy with the work in hand. Whilst I had a cup of tea she sat sewing at the sewing machine. Suddenly it jammed. She spent some time trying to un-jam it, and finally said to me: "Lance, do you know anything about sewing machines?" I replied: "I know nothing whatsoever!" I went over and also tried to un-jam her machine, but was unsuccessful! Then she said: "We have to ask our Father." With that she pointed to the floor and said: "Kneel!" I immediately knelt, and so did she next to the machine. She lifted up one hand and said: "Father, Lance, dear boy, and I have been having a wonderful time of fellowship about your Son. You know, dear Father, that I am an impractical lady, and I have lived my whole life in the art and cultural world: Something is wrong with this sewing machine and I have tried to put it right, but it has not worked. Lance, dear boy, knows nothing whatsoever about sewing machines, but he has tried and has also been unsuccessful. Now Father, we come to You, Lance, dear boy, and I, with one of Your promises, over which You have said: 'In Christ is the yea and through Him is the Amen, to your glory. And in Hebrews 1:14 it says: 'Are they not all ministering spirits, sent forth to do service for the sake of them that shall inherit salvation.' Lance, dear boy, and I, stand upon this promise. Send an angel now to put this sewing machine right." She bowed her head, but I had my eyes wide open, and out like organ stops, as big as saucers, looking for the angel! After quite a few minutes, I said: "Auntie, try it!" "Shush" she said, "give the angel time!" Suddenly she got up from her knees, and said: "Thank You, Father, You never fail," and pulled the stool under her and went straight on with her sewing.

Then I thought to myself: has an angel actually come into this room and put this sewing machine right? Has this little old sister, who many in the Church think is nuts, stood on a promise of the Word of God, and seen it fulfilled, and if she can, can I? It changed my life. In the Baptist Church we had many great and famous preachers come to speak, but it was Auntie Ella, with her living and simple faith who taught me that the Word was not just beautiful ideals, but a means through which we become partakers of the divine nature.

ELLEN RASSMUSSEN AND THE FULFILMENT OF HER COMMISSION

Here is another illustration of the absolute trustworthiness of the Word of God when the Holy Spirit applies it to personal situations. Many years later, I met a remarkable eighty-seven year old Danish sister in the Lord. Her name was Ellen Rassmussen. She told me that when she was eighteen, the Lord had told her that she was to go to Afghanistan and preach the Gospel. The problem was that Afghanistan was closed to the Gospel, and there was no possibility of entrance into that land. So she went to a place as near as possible to Afghanistan. At that time it was part of India; today it is an area on the border between Pakistan and Afghanistan. All through the years, she told me she stood on this word from the Lord. The years went by and the mission to which she belonged believed in the retirement of their workers at a certain age. Ellen however, believed that the Lord had commissioned her to go to Afghanistan. So instead of retirement, she took a small home near the border. She never retired, but went on with the work of the Gospel, and with her untiring intercession for Afghanistan.

One day, when she was eighty years of age, there was a knocking on her door, and when she opened it there stood a man clearly dressed in the Afghan manner, and in very special clothes that denoted he was in the employ of one of the highest families in that nation. He said: "Are you Ellen Rassmussen?" "Yes," she said, "I am." "Are you specialized as a nurse in eye troubles?" "Yes, I am" she said. The man said: "I am come from the King of Afghanistan to ask you in his name to come to Kabul to help nurse the crown prince who has serious eye problems." Thus at eighty years of age, the Lord fulfilled the commission He gave to Ellen Rassmussen when she was eighteen. From her work in Kabul, and with the King's authority and protection, a well known eye doctor and missionary, was asked to come to Afghanistan. From all of this, came an assembly of believers, many of whom remained faithful to martyrdom at the hands of the Taliban when the king was deposed decades later.

These two stories illustrate how faithful the Lord is to His Word. There is not a child of God who cannot have such experience. When we trust Him, and stand on His promises, He always fulfils them. The one essential necessity is to know that it really is the Lord who is speaking.

OUR AUTHORITY HAS TO BE DELEGATED AUTHORITY

All true divine authority is delegated authority; we are not authorized to throw our weight around as if we are the supreme authority. The Lord Jesus is the supreme authority, and under Him, and with Him, we are to exercise His authority. This requires that we know His mind and His will in any given matter or situation, before we can take any executive action. The idea that we can impose our will, or our ideas, on a matter without consulting the Lord, and that He then will support us, is utterly false and dangerous. There have been many tragedies amongst believers as a result of this mentality. Our authority is vested, and only vested in the Lord Jesus. As has been pointed out already, with us it is delegated authority.

Nevertheless, when the mind of the Lord has been revealed to us, kingship requires that we take action. It is interesting to note that whether as "kings" or as "a kingdom" or "kingship" a plurality is involved; it is a corporate matter and we act together in fellowship. This truth is of enormous practical importance! Sometimes it is one person's understanding that he or she is seeking to impose on us all. The real evidence that it is the Lord's mind and will, is when a number share the same witness. We come back again to the Lord's word: "If two of you shall agree on earth as touching anything that they shall ask, it shall be done for them of my Father who is in heaven" (Matthew 18:19). Those believers have been harmonized by the Spirit into one mind.

This kind of kingship in action, the taking of executive action in the Name of the Lord, requires that there be a certain nucleus of believers who are freewill offerings. They have made the Lord Jesus absolute Lord in their lives, and have laid down their self-life, and have become living sacrifices; they have also some experience of being fitly framed together, and of growing into a holy temple in the Lord. Where there is both this kind of personal and corporate experience, there can be the function of kingship. No believer, whoever he or she may be, can exercise authority, without genuine fellowship and a true walk with the Lord. Kingship requires a certain history; spiritual character, discipline, training, and instruction, are all necessary requirements, and all of them need time to be developed.

It is patently obvious from all of this that the greatest need is for those who are freewill offerings to come under the absolute Lordship of Jesus. The key to genuine executive action is to have an ear to hear what the Lord is saying. Without an understanding of the mind and will of the enthroned Lamb, we are left to throw our weight around, which often happens with disastrous results! All deception, delusion, and digression from the will and mind of the Head, begins with spiritual deafness. From this we understand that the paramount need in exercising authority is to have a "hearing ear," and to discern in any given situation what is the mind of the Lord.

THE NEPAL PRAYER MEETING

When I was a teenager and a few years old in the Lord, I became part of a prayer meeting for Nepal. At that time, Nepal was a closed kingdom to the Gospel; it was forbidden even to become a Christian. There were two sisters, Dr. O'Hanlon and Lucy Steele, who knew that the Lord had clearly called them to Nepal, but there was no possibility of entering the country. However the Lord had commanded them to go to Nepal; so they did the only thing they could do, which was to live as near as possible to Nepal on the mountains of the Indian side of the border.

Nearly everyone in the prayer meeting of which I was part was white haired and old, and those who were not white haired, in my arrogant view, were old! I was the only young person! The young people of the Church, used to say to me: "What in the world are you doing, going to that meeting of old white haired fogies?" I used to say: "We are praying that Nepal will open to the Gospel." "That will never happen in a thousand years," they said; "you are wasting your time, and beating your head on a brick wall."

I remember when the cable came to ask us to pray for Dr. O'Hanlon and Lucy Steele that they would have permission to go over the border and set up a clinic in

Nepal. It was real prayer, but nothing seemed to happen. However, we all continued to intercede in faith. Then suddenly the cable came from the two sisters: "We have been granted permission to go over the border tomorrow, and to set up a clinic in Nepal." I could hardly believe it, that I so young could have been part of a prayer meeting that had prayed for a national matter, and stood on the Word of God, and seen it come to fulfilment. From this humble beginning so much developed in Nepal. For me, it taught me that with God nothing is impossible!

PRIESTS UNTO GOD

There can be few higher callings than this calling of God to be priests unto Him. Every born again child of God is at their spiritual birth constituted a priest. We call this "the priesthood of all true believers." Since the Reformation it has been the official doctrine of Protestants. Priests are not an elite or an especial caste in the Church; but whether priests, or pastors, or even spiritual leaders, we have produced a system whereby certain especial people are elevated, and the rest sit and listen. It has become a denial of the truth of the "priesthood of all believers." The Apostle Peter in his first letter states: "Unto whom coming, a living stone, rejected indeed of men, but with God elect, precious, ye also as living stones, are built up a spiritual house, to be a holy priesthood, to offer up spiritual sacrifices acceptable to God through Jesus Christ" (1 Peter 2:4-5). Note carefully that this holy priesthood is made up of all the living stones and not a designated class! These holy priests are to offer up spiritual sacrifices. Peter even calls all those born of God "a royal priesthood."

The Apostle Paul, writing to the Church at Corinth, exclaims: "What is it then, brethren? When ye come together, each one hath a psalm, hath a teaching, hath a revelation, hath a tongue, hath an interpretation" (1 Corinthians 14:26). It is clear from this that he was speaking about the "priesthood of all believers." As the Holy Spirit leads, the believers were to contribute what they had from the Lord. All through the history of the Church, when there has been full and powerful spiritual life, there has been the functioning of the "priesthood of all believers." Long before the Reformation, when it became official doctrine, many of the movements of the Holy Spirit had been expressed in this manner. However, with the diminishing of spiritual life, certain people had to take the helm, and the rest were happy to sit and listen! As a result the practical outworking of "the priesthood of all believers" was seriously hampered, if not destroyed. In times of great renewal and revival, it bursts out again spontaneously; it cannot be restrained. Everyone who is spiritually alive shares what they have of the Lord Jesus.

CALLED TO BE INTERCESSORS

"In the day of His power, His people are freewill offerings." Those who are totally given to the Lord, and filled with His Spirit, become functioning priests, and are called to be intercessors. Under the Old Covenant, one of the main functions of being a priest was to be an intercessor. The word "intercession" has been seriously devalued in recent years; in much the same way as "being born again" has been devalued. It has been used as if it is merely petition. Intercession is the deepest form of prayer; it begins with the knowledge of the will of God for a nation, a person, or a problematic situation. The Holy Spirit conceives such intercession; it is a burden that comes from the enthroned Christ by the Holy Spirit into a believer, or a group of believers. Once it is conceived, there is no respite until it is birthed. The Apostle Paul speaks of this when he writes in the Galatian letter: "My little children, of whom I am again in travail until Christ be formed in you" (Galatians 4:19). Note carefully the word again; apparently Paul had travailed for the spiritual birth of these people. Now he was again in travail, and he uses a very strong word in Greek, "the agony of childbirth." That is true intercession! With such intercession, there is always an outcome and the burden is fulfilled.

The Lord Jesus declared: "If two of you shall agree on earth as touching anything that they shall ask, it shall be done for them of my Father who is in heaven. For where two or three are gathered together in my Name, there am I in the midst of them" (Matthew 18:19-20). This tremendous statement is rarely read as it should be as one single declaration. It is normally quoted in two sentences, which are not related to each other. The latter part of the statement is quoted as relating to any gathering together of Christians; and the former is quoted as a promise that if we agree to agree, the Lord will have to answer our prayer. In fact, it is one statement. Note carefully the little word for; it links the first part of the statement to the last. Many of us have been in meetings where someone at the front asks if there are any persons present who will agree with him in order that a prayer request is answered. It is of course extraordinary when we get Christians to agree, but the idea, that by such an agreement to agree, we can push the Lord into a corner and make Him answer in a way that He does not want to answer, is ridiculous!

The word agree in Greek is the word sumphoneo from which we get the English, "symphony" or "symphonize." When, however, we take the whole statement together, we discover that it is the Lord in the midst of at least two or three believers gathered "in His Name" who, by the Spirit of God, have been made of one mind in prayer. They have been harmonized; they have been brought into unanimity in that for which they are asking. They are members of the body of the Lord Jesus, and thus are praying in His Name. The burden on the heart of the Great Intercessor, the enthroned Messiah, has been brought by the Holy Spirit into the hearts of those two or three gathered in His Name on earth. When the intercession has been thus harmonized, the Lord Jesus said: "It shall be done for them of my Father who is in heaven." This turns a time of true intercession into an amazingly powerful and exciting time.

Many times in the prayer meetings at Halford House, in Richmond, Surrey, they became so exciting that newly saved young people would choose to come to the prayer meeting as a priority. It was clear that anything could happen in those times of intercession.

Of course, it was not that every time we prayed we immediately had the answer. It was true that sometimes the answer came the same night we prayed. On the other hand, we prayed every night for four months for the Lord to do something in Richmond, and in the Thames Valley. It resulted finally in the fellowship of believers meeting at Halford House. On another occasion we prayed for a world wide breaking in of the Holy Spirit into believers of all kinds of persuasions, that there would be a new and clear understanding of the Church as the body of Christ. It took every day of three years and one more year of praise for the answer to be won! After a year or two, we grew and reinstituted the Bible study for all, and especially the new believers who had been added to us. This took from 1961 to 1964.

THE POWER OF INTERCESSION

It was in the weekly prayer meeting of the Baptist Church in which I had been saved that I first became aware of the importance of prayer. Although most of the deacons, with some notable exceptions, did not attend the prayer meeting, saying that they were too busy with their businesses, or work. The pastor, Alan Redpath, was always there unless he was leading an evangelistic crusade. I still see him in my mind's eye kneeling on the wooden floor of the church hall. He would remain in that position during the whole prayer meeting.

It was, however, years later that I came to understand the power of intercession. It all began with two old and retired missionaries of the Egypt General

Mission. I knew them as Aunts. They were Alexandra Liblik and Kathleen Smythe. I had been very ill, and recovered. The Royal Air Force doctors told me that I had to get away from the Royal Air force and convalesce for some weeks. The superintendent's wife of the E.G.M in Isamailiya, Susan Hamill, said that she was sure that I could go and stay with these two missionaries, and that she would arrange it. She came back to me a little later saying that it was arranged and said: "Now you must be careful. These are very godly and pious missionaries, and you are young, full of life, and arrogant. You must be careful and respectful!"

Thus I came to know Auntie Alexandra, and Auntie Kathleen. My stay with them was to change my life. A few days went by, and I began to realize that something extraordinary was taking place in their home. A letter would come, or a phone call would be made, or a visitor came and I would hear Auntie Kathleen saying with a loud voice: "Alex, prayer!" With that the two of them vanished into the lounge and shut the door. I wondered what in the world was going on, because in the evening the phone would ring, and I would hear Auntie Kathleen exclaiming: "Hallelujah! Alex and I got the victory on that this midday." And then she would talk on with whoever phoned, on that occasion from Beirut. On another occasion they shared a letter from Algiers in the morning prayer, and by the evening they had a phone call to say that their prayer had been answered. I was eaten up with curiosity! What in the world went on in that lounge? However, they always said that I must rest and be still.

Then one day after about a week or more, Auntie Alexandra asked me: "Would you like to join us in prayer?" I kept a very cool exterior, and said in my best British manner: "That would be very nice." However, I had been dying to be invited to join them and see what happened in that lounge! I was not prepared for what happened! They took another letter which they had received and translated it from the Arabic for me. It was all about a dreadful Church situation in Damanhur, in Egypt. Auntie Alexandra said to me: "Do you understand?" And I replied, "Yes, I think I do." Then she said: "Have either of you got any Scripture that we might stand on?" Auntie Kathleen said: "Yes, I have," and quoted a verse from Obadiah. I had never heard or seen anything like it. I did not even know where Obadiah was in the Old Testament, let alone how it had bearing on the Church situation in Damanhur! We then got on our knees. The two of them prayed short prayers, never very long. Backwards and forwards it went, whilst I was struck with dumbness. Then suddenly Auntie Alex said: "Do you think we have broken through?" Auntie Kathleen said: "No, not yet, we have further to go." And so they went on.

The only way I can describe it was that they were like men manning the guns on a battleship. To me they both had their helmets on, and were trying to get the enemy plane in their sights until finally they could shoot it out of the sky. Suddenly Auntie Kathleen would start praising the Lord, and so would Auntie Alexandra. I had to go and lie down on my bed. I had never seen anything like it! I had been in a number of very good and powerful prayer meetings, but nothing came anywhere near those two incredible sisters. That evening the news came through by phone; there had been an amazing reconciliation between the main protagonists in the problems in Damanhur, and they were reconciled with many tears.

For me it was an introduction to another dimension of intercession. I became aware that these two old sisters were like a spiritual intelligence service, or a spiritual security service, watching the whole Middle East from Fez in Morocco, to Baghdad in Iraq, from Aden in the Yemen, to Khartoum in the Sudan. I realized that more could be accomplished by such intercession than a thousand diplomatic Christians seeking to solve the problems. It also came to me that such intercession required at least two believers, fused together; who had also some spiritual maturity. They were a spiritual symphony, harmonized, and under the leadership of the Holy Spirit as the conductor. Truly they brought the Kingdom of God to bear on many impossible situations; they caused the will of God, to be done, as in heaven, so on earth.

These two old sisters came to mean much to me. I asked them on one occasion: "How many people have you led to the Lord in your service in Egypt?" Auntie Alexandra held one hand up with five fingers outstretched. In my youthful arrogance I exclaimed: "Is it worth it, fifty years for five people?" Quietly, she said: "There will come a day when multitudes and multitudes of Muslims will come to the Lord Jesus, gloriously saved." It took their lifetime, and almost mine, for those words to be realized. More Muslims today are coming to Christ than at any time since the advent of Islam in the 7th century. It is much due to the intercession of people like Alexandra Liblik and Kathleen Smythe, and Lillias Trotter. They, and many others before them who have died, died in faith not receiving the promise of a great harvest from Islam. They have prayed it into being, and their works follow them!

<h2 style="text-align:center">THE SEX BOUTIQUE</h2>

This story illustrates how a group of saved people, joined to the Head, at God's right hand can see something done on this fallen earth. There was a woman in Hamburg, Germany who had set up a whole string of sex boutiques across Germany, Holland, and Scandinavia. Finally she had decided she would come to Britain, and chose Richmond, Surrey, as the first place for her English sex boutique chain in Britain. Someone came in one day, and told us that opposite the railway station a sex boutique had opened. So we began to ask the Lord what we should do about it and we had a marvellous time as the whole fellowship came together in prayer. God gave us certain Scriptures which we stood on, and we came to a certain night when we felt that the Lord had given us the victory. We began to praise the Lord that the sex boutique was finished.

The next day, Margaret Trickey, who looked after Halford House, went out shopping. She came back in quite a state and laughed so much that we could not get anything out of her. For a while she just stood there leaning on the doorpost giggling. Finally, she said: "The sex boutique, the sex boutique." So I said, "Margaret, you have not been in the sex boutique, have you?" Then she said, "No, I have not been in the sex boutique." But she could not get out what she wanted to say. At last I said: "Tell us what it is; tell us what has happened." She said, "The sex boutique has blown up."

Now the night before we had been at prayer for it, and some of the brothers who had been saved, who had been juvenile delinquents and in youth prisons, had all been praying their hearts out about this. Finally, I had gathered up all the prayer and said; "Lord, we take this sex boutique and we blow it up in the Name of the Lord. Out, completely gone!" So Margaret said: "It has gone; all four floors have collapsed in a heap." Then she laughed some more. And I said: "Margaret, it is not a laughing matter; the police will be around in no time." We had written a letter to the Mayor of Richmond telling him that we were disgusted that he could have allowed a sex boutique to be opened in Richmond. He had written back and said he could not do anything about it, but we should write to the Superintendent of the police. So we had written to the Superintendent of the police, who had then written to us and said he could not do anything about it. We should write to the mayor. So we knew we were not going to get anywhere in this. Then I thought that maybe the police superintendent would send someone around, not to me, but to speak to some of these boys whom he had known formerly. Obviously he was going to say to them: "Do you know anyone in the fellowship who would blow up a sex boutique?" I said: "Margaret one of them is bound to say that one of the leaders prayed, 'Lord, blow up the sex boutique.' We are going to be in trouble over this matter." Then Margaret collected herself, and said that she had gone to the shop next door to the sex boutique and spoken with them, and they were very angry about what had happened to it. They said it was the gas fire heating that had blown up and that furthermore they were not insured. That was the end of the sex boutique chain. That is what God can do in a prayer meeting when we learn to stand on the Word of God, and it is a corporate matter. Of course today, many years later, sex boutiques are in many places, but this story reveals what can be done through intercession.

INTERCESSION INFLUENCING A GOVERNMENT

At one time many years ago, before Britain became part of the European Union, there was a battle over whether she should join it. At Halford House we had a week of prayer about the matter. It seemed quite clear that, behind the scenes, the British government had decided to join the European Union. Everything pointed to that conclusion. However, we sought the Lord as to what was His mind. The day that it was announced that the British government had applied to join the European Union; we had an amazing prayer time. We felt that the Lord gave us the victory, although everything seemed to point to Britain's acceptance by the Europeans.

Then in that evening prayer meeting, an old brother and one of the elders had a Word from the Lord: "The lot is cast into the lap; But the whole disposing thereof is of the Lord" (Proverbs 16:33). Everyone rose to it. It was amazing to us that during the night and the early morning, President De Gaulle of France vetoed it. He said that Britain's destiny lay with the English speaking peoples of the Dominions, and of the United States, and not with Europe. We praised the Lord.

Years later the whole matter rose up again. This time, however, the Lord told us that we would go into the European Union, and it was a judgment upon Britain, but out of every country in the European Union would come multitudes of saved people.

TWO STORIES OF INTERCESSION IN THE YOM KIPPUR WAR OF 1973

Delivered from Destruction by Intercession

This story illustrates how a nation can be delivered from its enemy by intercession. In the Yom Kippur war of 1973, in November a number of us met for prayer in a special place in what we called the bunker. The situation for Israel was extremely grave and the war was not going well for her. Some three thousand young men had already died, and some of the greatest tank battles in military history up to that point in time were being fought in the Sinai. When we began to pray, the Hashemite Kingdom of Jordan, ruled by King Hussein, had not joined in the war. Israel was fighting on two fronts—the North Eastern front with Syria and the Southern front with Egypt. Jordan had the longest border of all with Israel. If she had come in, Israel could have lost the war.

We met for prayer; I remember it well. A way into

our time of prayer, Colonel Orde Dobbie suddenly broke into the prayer and said, "Would you all please judge this; three times I have clearly had the same picture. I have seen the mountains of Moab and clouds have come down each time and blotted them out. Does this have some meaning for our prayer or is it my crazy mind?" Orde was a military man and came from a family with a long history of serving in the British army. His father was Lt. General Sir William Dobbie, the defender of Malta in the Second World War. His cousin was General Orde Wingate, often called the Father of the Israel Defence Forces. Orde Dobbie was not given to sentimentality or emotionalism! We were quiet for a moment, and then one brother said, "I think the Lord has given this vision to direct us to pray that Jordan should stay out of this war." We all had a witness that this was true and we immediately took it up in prayer. If I remember properly, we began to pray that the Lord would confuse the Jordanians and keep them out of the war. One person had the Scripture about the Lord sending a lying spirit to confuse the enemy. We stood on this Scripture and others in much prayer until quite suddenly we felt that the battle was won in the heavenlies. We began then to praise the Lord. Jordan never did enter that war, and for that she was roundly criticized by her Arab neighbors.

Months afterwards I was back in England, and my mother called up to my bedroom and said "Lance, come down quickly; King Hussein is on the television, and he is talking about the Yom Kippur war." I came down quickly to hear the interviewer saying: "Your majesty, everyone blames you for the defeat of the Arabs in this war because you never joined in." King Hussein said: "We had made the decision to join Egypt and Syria in this war, but suddenly we became confused. The problem was did we have sufficient air cover to allow us to enter the war? We did not, and therefore we could not commit ourselves." The Lord had answered prayer!

AVERTING A NUCLEAR CATASTROPHE

This is another illustration from the Yom Kippur war of genuine intercession which can change the course of events nationally and even internationally. The war was going very badly in the Yom Kippur war. We were pleading with the Lord that He would do something. Then suddenly this dear brother who had grown up with the Royal family in Holland began to speak. His father was personal secretary, first to Queen Wilhelmina of the Netherlands, and secondly to Queen Juliana. He said: "I do not know whether I should divulge this, but our ambassador told me yesterday that there is intelligence information that the Soviets have brought a warship out of the Black Sea and sailed it across the Eastern Mediterranean to Alexandria. The Soviet soldiers are dressed in Egyptian soldiers' clothes. They have set up quickly a missile system in Alexandria, and their plan is to fire a nuclear missile on Tel Aviv. When it is fired, they will disown that they had any part in it; that it was completely an Egyptian plan. After the missile had been fired and Tel Aviv was no more, they would say, "Now we had better have a Middle East peace conference." This conference would not have been at all sympathetic to Israel.

We believed that this knowledge which our brother had divulged was really of God, and we all got on our knees. There were two sisters who were with us, Gladys Roberts and Kitty Morgan, working in Ramallah amongst Arab girls. They went through the war years with Rees Howells in those amazing times of intercession, which basically determined the course of the Second World War. They had woken up in the previous night and felt that the Lord had said that His enemy was planning something terrible for Israel. Interestingly, Samuel Howells, the son of Rees Howells, thousands of miles away in Wales had also been woken up that same night, and the Lord had said to him: "Call the Bible college to prayer. My enemy is seeking to bring in Armageddon before its time."

We went to prayer. I remember that the Lord gave me a strange feeling about a certain Scripture which said: "The hidden things will be made known." We stood upon it. After many hours of prayer we came to the conclusion that the Lord had answered and we began to praise Him. It was not long afterwards that someone came in and said: "Have you heard the latest news? President Nixon has called a worldwide emergency alert for all American forces. His intelligence service has picked up that there are certain Soviet troops in Southern Russia being geared up for nuclear or chemical warfare, and being readied to fly to Egypt." After the alert, the Russian warship packed up its nuclear equipment and sailed back across the Eastern Mediterranean.

The world had come very near to a nuclear exchange, not just relating to Israel, but to the superpowers, which would have been a worldwide catastrophe. It had been averted by the Lord. Can you believe that God could use twelve very ordinary people in intercession and executive action to avert an international and catastrophic conflict?

THE CALLING OF THOSE WHO ARE FREEWILL OFFERINGS TO HIM

From these illustrations of the power in genuine intercession, we can see what a tremendous calling is ours to be kings and priests. We are to be involved in the fulfilment of His purpose for this earth. Even if this earth is fallen and filled with evil spirits, ruled by spiritual principalities and powers and world rulers of this present darkness, the end of their influence and power is in sight! It is only a matter of time before, at the word of the Father, the Son returns with great power and glory. In the meantime, we are to be involved in both the exercise of Divine authority, which originates in the enthroned Christ, and the kind of intercession which springs from Him. This calling is awesome and humbling! Practically it begins with believers who are freewill offerings in the day of His power. The Lord does not force or impose this calling on all His children, but only on those who are prepared to be living sacrifices. Such freely offered sacrifice is our spiritually intelligent service and worship.

We are still in the day of His power, but where today are those who are the freewill offerings? The work of the Lord, the building of the Church, the spiritual growth of those born of the Spirit, all require the kind of action we have been considering. The paramount need as the World more and more deeply moves into pagan and demonic darkness is for the triumph of the enthroned Lamb to be registered with impact and reality. We are in the shadow of the coming of the anti-Christ, but that is no reason to be cast down or depressed. The Lord Jesus is with us all the days until the consummation of the age. His victory needs to be realized no matter how dark or difficult the days, whether it is personal or family, or local, national, or even worldwide.

Satan and the powers of darkness cannot dislodge the Messiah from the throne and are unable to nullify His triumph. We are called with no lesser calling than to be with the Lord Jesus as kings and priests, and to see His total victory registered again and again until He returns. As it is written: "These shall war against the Lamb, and the Lamb shall overcome them, for He is Lord of Lords, and King of Kings; and they also shall overcome that are with Him, called and chosen and faithful" (Revelation 17:14).

Chapter 9

In the Day of His Army

Psalm 110:1-5—The Lord saith unto my Lord, Sit thou at my right hand,
Until I make thine enemies the footstool of thy feet.
The Lord will send forth the rod of thy strength out of Zion:
Rule thou in the midst of thine enemies.
Thy people are freewill-offerings
In the day of thy power,
In the beauty of holiness:
Out of the womb of the morning
Thy youth are to thee as dew.
The Lord hath sworn, and will not repent;
Thou art a priest for ever
After the order of Melchizedek.
The Lord at thy right hand
Will strike through kings in the day of his wrath.

Ephesians 6:10-14a, 17-19—Finally, be strong in the Lord, and in the strength of his might. Put on the whole armour of God, that ye may be able to stand against the wiles of the devil. For our wrestling is not against flesh and blood, but against the principalities, against the powers, against the world rulers of this darkness, against the spiritual hosts of wickedness in the heavenly places. Wherefore take up the whole armour of God, that ye may be able to withstand in the evil day, and, having done all, to stand. Stand therefore

...And take the helmet of salvation, and the sword of the Spirit, which is the word of God: with all prayer and supplication praying at all seasons in the Spirit, and watching thereunto in all perseverance and supplication for all the saints, and on my behalf, that utterance may be given unto me in opening my mouth, to make known with boldness the mystery of the gospel ...

With this chapter this book comes to its conclusion. We have been dealing with a very complex and difficult subject but have sought to be as lucid and simple as possible in the explanation of it. There is no doubt at all that the Messiah Jesus is seated. He has won, and Satan cannot dethrone Him or frustrate God's purpose for Him. This is proclaimed not merely in Psalm 110 but everywhere in the New Testament. The Father has said to the Son: "Sit thou at my right hand, until I make thine enemies the footstool of thy feet." The question we have to ask is, will He do this work alone, or are the redeemed in some measure involved in it?

We should note that although the Lord Jesus has won and sat down in triumph, there is a continuing warfare. Mark the words: "Make thine enemies the footstool of thy feet," and "Rule thou in the midst of thine enemies." It is obvious that the enthronement of the Lamb has not rid us of these enemies. Indeed they are more violent than ever!

Whilst the Devil cannot touch the Lord Jesus, he can touch us, seeking to divert us from God's will, and thus immobilize us. Satan and his cohorts are the implacable enemies of God and of the Messiah; they are also the enemies of all who have been delivered: "Out of the power of darkness and translated into the kingdom of the Son of his love …" (Colossians 1:13). Satan rages against the living Church, against those who are totally devoted to the Lord Jesus. At times this battle reaches incredibly intense heights!

Attention has already been drawn to the fact that it is not the general and huge concourse of those born of God, who are described in Psalm 110:3, but those who are freewill offerings. They are a kind of first fruits of the harvest, the first born ones in the great company of the redeemed. In what practical manner are they involved in the fulfilment of God's purpose? That they have some actual involvement in the realization and enforcement of the victory and triumph of the Messiah seems reasonably clear from a careful reading of the book of Acts. Note carefully the statement at the beginning of that book and underline it: "The former treatise I made, O Theophilus, concerning all that Jesus began both to do and to teach, until the day in which He was received up …" (Acts 1:1-2). The Gospel of Luke is the record of what Jesus began to do; the book of Acts is the record of the continuation of what He is doing through His body. The book of Acts has no clear conclusion; it is open ended. The story is still being recorded of those who are realizing and enforcing His total triumph in this fallen world.

It is important fully to understand the words: "In the day of thy power." The Hebrew "Hayil," can be translated, "strength," or "wealth," or "army." The Jewish Publication Society Bible actually translates these words as: "In the day of thy warfare." When the

Messiah Jesus finally sat down at God's right hand, He had won; the finished work of our salvation was confirmed by His enthronement. At that point He had poured forth the promise of the Spirit, who by His Presence in us and with us, makes all that was accomplished in that finished work a reality. It was truly the day of His power! The warfare however is not over, it has moved from the Lord Jesus to those who are redeemed and alive on this fallen earth. In that sense, it is the day of thy warfare.

Those people who are freewill offerings in the "day of His army," are volunteers not conscripts. The army of the Messiah Jesus is a volunteer army! There is no doubt about the violent warfare into which we have been introduced by our new birth. Although the Messiah, our Lord Jesus has won and sat down, and the Father has ratified it, Satan and his cohorts refuse to accept the fact. They still believe that they can frustrate God's purpose by undermining and nullifying all that the Lord Jesus has won for us. It is astonishing that the only way, in fact, to negate the effects of His finished work and enthronement is the passivity and disbelief of the Church and of Christian believers! Even Satan himself cannot nullify the triumph of Jesus.

It is for this reason that the Apostle Paul writing to Timothy appeals to him: "Suffer hardship with me, as a good soldier of Christ Jesus. No soldier on service entangleth himself in the affairs of this life; that he may please him who enrolled him as a soldier" (II Timothy 2:3-4).

Or again: "This charge I commit unto thee, my child

Timothy, according to the prophecies which led the way to thee, that by them thou mayest war the good warfare ..." (1 Timothy 1:18). And again: "Fight the good fight of the faith, lay hold on the life eternal, whereunto thou wast called" (1 Timothy 6:12).

Or once again in Paul's own testimony: "I have fought the good fight, I have finished the course, I have kept the faith ..." (II Timothy 4:7). From these quotations it is clear, in spite of the fact that Jesus has won, we who belong to the Lord are in a battle, sometimes incredibly intense.

THE VOLUNTEER ARMY OF THE LORD

Is this volunteer army of the Lord merely ceremonial, reserved for state occasions, or is it a genuine army? If the Father has said to the Son "sit thou at My right hand until I make thine enemies the footstool of thy feet," will He do this work alone? If He is working totally alone, why then are we called to fight the good fight of faith, to war the good warfare, and to suffer hardship as good soldiers of Christ Jesus? Is it merely personal and only related to our individual Christian life?

When the Apostle wrote to Timothy and said "war the good warfare," that warfare must surely have had much to do with the planting of Churches in many localities. It is interesting to note that Paul in his first letter to Timothy writes about this warfare and then goes on to write about intercession: "I exhort therefore, first of all, that supplications, prayers, intercessions, thanksgivings, be made for all men; for kings and all that are in high place; that we may lead a tranquil and quiet life in all godliness and gravity. This is good and acceptable in the sight of God our Saviour; who would have all men to be saved" (1 Timothy 2:1-4 cp. 1:18).

It is obvious that most of these kings and men in high places at that time were not believers. Some of them were positively evil and violently opposed to the Word of God and the spread of the Gospel. Paul emphasizes the priority of praying for both imperial and national leaders. It is not relating merely to politics that is his concern, but of the spread of the Gospel and the planting and building up of the Church. There were imperial situations, as well as national and local problems, that were humanly speaking mountainous obstacles in the way of the progress of the Gospel and the planting of Churches. If the purpose of God was to be fulfilled, these satanic strongholds or fortresses needed to be cast down.

It is surely concerning these situations and problems that Paul wrote to the Church in Corinth: "For though we walk in the flesh, we do not war according to the flesh (for the weapons of our warfare are not of the flesh, but mighty before God to the casting down of strongholds), casting down imaginations, and every high thing that is exalted against the knowledge of God, and bringing every thought into captivity to the obedience of Christ" (II Corinthians 10:3-5).

We should note the manner in which Paul writes of this warfare. It is related to issues more powerful and influential than personal matters—casting down, or hurling down strongholds; casting down high things exalted against the knowledge of God, and casting down imaginations or speculations. This covers so much in fallen world society. Humanism, Darwinism, Marxism, Nazism and Maoism are all "high things exalted against the knowledge of God." They are thoughts which have led to much death and blood letting. The whole atmosphere of the Apostle's words describes continuous and violent spiritual warfare.

We should carefully note firstly, that this is spiritual warfare, and not to be conducted by the energy, the emotions, or the wisdom of the flesh. Secondly, we have weapons of our warfare which are only operative in the Presence of God: "Mighty before God" or "Mighty in the Presence of God." They do not operate by our own will, or reasoning ability, or our natural strength. Thirdly, there are satanic strongholds and fortresses which block any progress in the work of the Gospel, or of the building of the Church, and have to be cast down!

The fact of the matter is that by God given faith every advance which has been made, and every victory won, is through the realization of the triumph of the Lord Jesus. This has been through men and women who have left all, become living sacrifices, and in total devotion to the Messiah, have given themselves to Him. They have been true soldiers of the Lord Jesus, "volunteers in the day of His army."

THE INTERCESSION OF THE ONE HUNDRED AND TWENTY

It has been a very great blessing to me to have been associated with a company of believers who were greatly used of the Lord in the Second World War. It was through Norman Grubb that I came into fellowship with them. Most of them are now home with the Lord. It was in 1939 and at the outbreak of that war, that these one hundred and twenty would be missionaries were caught in the Bible College of Wales, led by Rees Howells. They were nearly all in their twenties. Since they were accepted candidates for mission work, they were exempted by the British government from military service. They did not know what to do at the outbreak of war and sought the Lord. They decided to stay together and pray.

The story of their intercession and prayer warfare has gone all round the world. In days when there was censorship of news they sought the Lord, and He gave them unbelievable spiritual discernment and intelligence. They prayed that the Nazi advance in North Africa would fail and be turned back; it was. They prayed that Egypt would not fall to the Nazis; it did not. They prayed that Nazi Germany would not invade Great Britain; not only did they not invade Britain, but were led by a lying spirit and the false advice of a guru to attack the Soviet Union. It was the longest battle front in history. They prayed that in Volgograd, the advance of the Nazi armies would be halted; it was a battle that lasted years in which three divisions of the German army were destroyed. We know the place as Stalingrad. It was in fact the end of Nazi Germany, although the war went on for some more years. They prayed that the Japanese would never take India; they never did. They prayed that the U.S.A would enter the war; they did.

It sounds simple when it is written down, but these

battles, and many more that I have not mentioned, were occasions for intense spiritual warfare that lasted for days if not weeks. They stood on the word that the Lord gave them, until their prayer turned into victory, and praise. Although quite a few know this incredible story, it is generally speaking a hidden one from the world at large. God used these dear ones to determine the course of that war and particularly the survival of the Jewish people. In the spring of 1948 they took up the battle for the recreation of Israel. When all seemed lost, they had the word of the Lord, and stood on it until they felt that they had won the victory. All did seem lost, since in the United Nations there was then, as now, a built in majority against Israel. Suddenly, some days after they felt that they had won the battle, the Soviet Union switched its course and decided for its own reasons, to vote for the recreation of the State of Israel; as a result all the communist satellite nations immediately switched their vote, and there was a majority for the recognition of the right of Israel to be a state amongst the states of the world. It was the 14th May 1948. It was a miracle prophesied in the Word of God. Yet this group of intercessors prayed for that which was already prophesied, and prayed it into being. A miracle of no small proportions had been born, and Israel had become again a nation amongst the nations.

We should note that these one hundred and twenty were freewill offerings in the day of His power. They were a volunteer army. They understood that the triumph of the Lord had to be applied and realized even on a worldwide and international level. Some of the stories rehearsed to me, by those who were present in those sessions of intercession, were unbelievable. The fruit of their intercession and executive action is part of history. As Daniel of old, they had seen what the purpose of God was, how it applied to their contemporary world, and they prayed it into being.

THE SUPREME CHARACTERISTIC OF HIS SOLDIERS

Babes or kindergarten children, or even adolescents, cannot be soldiers; it requires some kind of growth, of discipline, and of training. This helps us to understand the words: "In the day of His army, his people are volunteers." He does not forcefully impose this duty on those whom He saves, but waits for them to give up all right to themselves, to become living sacrifices, and to enter His army freely as volunteers. The Old Testament expression "the Lord of hosts is with us," has much deeper meaning when it is understood as the "Commander of the heavenly armies is with us." These armies which the Lord commands are both angelic and human!

The human army requires much instruction, training and discipline. It begins with the surrender of our will to His will. For all of us, this is the first and most difficult obstacle to overcome; but from the winning of this first battle, everything else flows. In any army we have to learn how to take orders! It is not an easy lesson to learn; our own will is the problem. However, we cannot give orders if we cannot take and obey them!

When C.T Studd was dying he said to his son-in-law, Norman Grubb, "I have not been the easiest of men, but

In the Day of His Army

this I can say, of all that He has commanded me to do, that all I have done." The Apostle John, in one sense, summed up C.T. Studd's life and ministry, when he said: "And the world passeth away, and the lust thereof: but he that doeth the will of God abideth for ever" (1 John 2:17). The supreme characteristic of this volunteer army is the surrender of the will to His will.

F. B. Meyer was deeply impressed and moved when C.T. Studd, as a young Cambridge graduate, spoke at Melbourne Hall, in Leicester, England, of which Dr. Meyer was then the pastor. C.T. Studd, with six others, was going out as missionaries to China. After he had spoken, F.B. Meyer asked him: "What is the secret of your life, and ministry?" For a few moments C.T. Studd was silent, and then he said: "The secret is that I have surrendered my will totally to God." Out of that surrender of his will, grew the largest missionary fellowship in the world—"The Worldwide Evangelization Crusade." He was a grain of wheat which fell into the ground and died and has truly borne much fruit! To enter the Lord's volunteer army and be enrolled requires one to be a freewill offering, to die to one's self and to live totally for Him. As the Apostle Paul testified: "For to me to live is Christ, and to die is gain" (Philippians 1:21).

THE BURDEN OF THE APOSTLE PAUL FOR EPHESUS

Our attention has already been drawn to the manner in which Paul concludes his Ephesian letter. It is generally recognized that in the New Testament the Ephesian letter of the Apostle, is the high tide water

187

mark of the revelation of God's Eternal Purpose. The Holy Spirit enabled the Apostle to put into writing a definition and an exposition of that which was in the heart and mind of God before the dawn of time, before even anything in the universe had been created. He states: "He made known to us the mystery of His will, according to His kind intention which He purposed in Him with a view to an administration suitable to the fullness of the times, that is, the summing up of all things in Christ, things in the heavens and things upon the earth" (Ephesians 1:9-10 NASB). This Eternal Purpose of God was and is centered in the Lord Jesus, whom He intended to be the summing up of all things. Without the Lord Jesus there is no Eternal Purpose as far as God is concerned!

With the fall of man that purpose was seriously contradicted. Satan had won a major victory, and it seemed as if the purpose of God was frustrated. The coming of the Lord Jesus into this world heralded a New Day, a New Man, and a New Creation. From the moment He was born in Bethlehem, until He died at Calvary, Satan fought to annihilate any possibility of a Divine victory, but failed. The finished work of the Lord Jesus on the cross marked the end of Satan's domination of this world. His resurrection, ascension, and glorification were the confirmation that Satan had been defeated; He had lost the battle! The enthroned Messiah, at God's right hand is the guarantee that His triumph will finally be registered in every part of this universe, and particularly on this fallen earth.

We who are alive at this point in time, and have

been saved by the grace of God, are living between the absolute triumph of the enthroned Lamb and His return to this earth in great power and glory. We are not only saved, but called to be kings and priests in fellowship with Him. We find ourselves in a furious battle! The Devil can do nothing about the enthronement of the Lord Jesus, and thus he vents his fury and wrath on those who belong to the Lord Jesus, and who are alive on this earth. It is in the vain hope that he might still frustrate the Eternal Purpose of God. Therefore, the great need is to learn how to stand in the triumph of the seated Christ. This was the Apostle's heavy burden for the Church at Ephesus, which had been entrusted by God with so much revelation and understanding.

BE STRONG IN THE LORD

It is of vital importance to recognize how the Apostle Paul concluded his Ephesian letter. We would have thought he would have exhorted us to go on, or to have arranged teaching conferences, or "seeking" meetings, or evangelistic crusades, all of which would have been valuable and right. Instead he urges us: "Be strong in the Lord and in the strength of His might" and to "put on the whole armour of God, that ye may be able to stand against the wiles of the Devil" (Ephesians 6:10-11). Carefully note, firstly that he warns us to put on the whole armour of God, not part of the armour, but the "whole" armour. Secondly he warns us to be aware of the stratagems and plans of the Devil.

It is quite clear that the apostle equates being "strong in the Lord and in the strength of His might" with putting on the whole armour of God. His mention of "armour" reveals that we are in a great spiritual war. You do not go to parties or banquets in full armour; it is to do with warfare. Immediately he writes: "Wrestling is not against flesh and blood, but against the principalities, against the powers, against the world-rulers of this darkness, against the spiritual hosts of wickedness in the heavenly places" (Ephesians 6:12). He then reemphasises this matter by saying: "Wherefore take up the whole armour of God, that ye may be able to withstand in the evil day, and, having done all, to stand" (6:13). Note again firstly that there is an "evil day" when apparently the Devil seems to have the upper hand and everything goes his way. All of us have known such days. Secondly, we are to take up the whole armour of God that in such a day of evil we may be able to withstand. Thirdly, Paul then goes on again to make abundantly clear that it is not one or two pieces of armour which we need, but the whole (see vv 14-17). He carefully describes each piece of the entire armour we are to put on, all of which is Christ.

THE INTENSE WARFARE OVER EPHESUS

Paul declares that this intense spiritual warfare is centered on the capacity and ability to understand practically the full purpose of God for the Church and the believer. He exhorts those who are functioning members of the body of Christ: "Take ... the sword of the Spirit, which is the word of God: with all prayer and supplication praying at all seasons in the Spirit, and watching thereunto in all perseverance and supplication for all the saints, and on my behalf, that utterance may be given unto me in opening of my mouth, to make known with boldness the mystery of the gospel" (Ephesians 6:17-19). Paul's heavy burden for the Church at Ephesus was that they needed to understand intercession and executive action. There needed to be those in that assembly who knew in experience what it was to be kings and priests unto God, or they would lose all that God had given them. The enemy would come in and would rob, and spoil, and destroy, unless there was the kind of intercession and kingship which protected the Lord's interests in that assembly. It was as if the Apostle was stating that the people of God, however much they understood of God's Eternal Purpose, would lose everything! They had to learn how to stand, to withstand, and having done all to stand in the full armour of God within His revealed purpose. Otherwise the enemy would leave them as monuments to a past, remarkable spiritual history. In order to come through this intense spiritual warfare and win, they would have to stand in the triumph of the enthroned Lamb, until it was practically realized in their circumstances.

STAND, WITHSTAND, AND HAVING DONE ALL TO STAND

It is of the utmost importance to understand that in the conclusion of this letter, Paul did not write about "fighting," "going forward," or "retreating," but only of standing and withstanding. This has to be the strangest way to win a battle! He even re-emphasizes this by writing "and having done all, to stand. Stand therefore

191

..." Since he writes in his other letters about "fighting the good fight," "warring the warfare," it is the more arresting that he only speaks of "standing" in the conclusion of this amazing letter. Has Paul revised his thinking, or changed his mind? Certainly not! He meant that standing, withstanding, and having done all to continue to stand, is the focal point of this warfare. It is the way we are meant to fight the good fight of faith, to war the good warfare! Satan, by pressure and stress, intends to make us withdraw, or take another position, or at the very least compromise and negotiate with him.

It is standing within the revealed purpose of God which is the key to overcoming. When in the fiercest part of the battle we learn to withstand, neither going forward, or backward, or sideways, but standing, then we experience the fulfilment of God's will and purpose for the Church, for the work of God, and for the individual believer.

Those who can thus stand in God's purpose have obviously been enlightened by the Spirit of God through His Word as to what is that purpose. Now they must learn not to retreat from it, or to go overboard on it, or get into strange doctrines about it, but to stand. In this way the battle will be won! If this especial Church at Ephesus could lose that which God had revealed to them, then what about us? The history of the Church furnishes us with vivid illustrations of this. So much of that which God revealed and did in the first generation of any move of God, was normally lost in the third or fourth, and succeeding generations. What had once been alive, functioning, full of spiritual activity and power, faithfully holding the Testimony of Jesus, within decades was a graveyard, full of monuments to past glory. This was Paul's warning to the Church at Ephesus. Stand uncompromised within the purpose and will of God, or lose everything!

THE SWORD OF THE SPIRIT

The triumph of the enthroned Lamb signifies that everything we need has been won for us! It is the assurance that whatever is needed for the protection of His work amongst us, for the enlightenment of the redeemed concerning His purpose, and for the practical building up of His body, is available through the person and work of the Holy Spirit. Now as kings and priests, it is necessary that the Spirit arms us with the promises and statements of the Word of God as weapons of our warfare, as the sword of the Spirit.

For this reason the Apostle declares that in the battle for the fulfilment of the purpose of God in Ephesus, and indeed anywhere, we must have the right weapons: "And take … the sword of the Spirit, which is the word of God: with all prayer and supplication praying at all seasons in the Spirit, and watching thereunto in all perseverance and supplication for all the saints." Upon this taking of the sword of the Spirit in intercession and executive action, the practical outworking of the whole purpose of God is dependant.

The sad fact is that the Church at Ephesus never rose to the occasion, and truly did become a monument to past glory. Through the long story of the living Church, there are many other examples, which furnish us with much from which to learn. It seems as if the Head of the Church is uninterested in keeping alive anything which no longer represents or expresses Him. He would rather take the initiative by the Holy Spirit, and start again. It is the story of the pilgrim Church.

THE LORD'S REMEMBRANCERS

We are called by the Head of the Church to be watchmen. We need to know what the mind and will of the Head is in any given matter, and to receive from Him by the Spirit the Word of God applied to the situations we face. Then we must learn to stand, to withstand, and having done all to stand within His will and on the Word which He has applied to our situation or problem. We have to learn the simple lesson that we must continue to stand and withstand, until we experience victory.

This is amazingly illustrated in the Word of the Lord to Zion in Isaiah 62: "I have set watchmen upon thy walls, O Jerusalem; they shall never hold their peace day nor night: ye that are the Lord's remembrancers, take ye no rest, and give Him no rest, till He establish, and till He make Jerusalem a praise in the earth" (Verses 6-7).

The Messiah Himself had already revealed His will, in declaring: "For Zion's sake will I not hold My peace, and for Jerusalem's sake I will not rest, until her righteousness go forth as brightness, and her salvation as a lamp that burneth" (Isaiah 62:1). The Lord reveals plainly His sovereign purpose. "For Zion's sake I will not hold My peace ...I will not rest ... until." He even explains His desire for Zion, that she should be a glorious testimony to the nations of the earth. Over this burden He says that He will not hold His peace, nor will He rest until it is fulfilled.

We know that the Messiah is enthroned at the right hand of God, and has won, and that the Father has committed into His hands all authority and power in heaven and on earth. We also know that Satan is unable to dethrone the Lord Jesus or to frustrate what He purposes. Why should He need our involvement in the execution of His purpose? The total triumph of the Lord Jesus and the placing by the Father of His enemies under His feet is surely a matter between the Father and the Son only.

Why then does the Messiah use the exact same words with which He has described His own intercession and burden for Zion, when speaking to the watchmen He has set upon the walls of Jerusalem? "They shall never hold their peace day nor night: ye that are the Lord's remembrancers, take ye no rest, and give Him no rest until He establish until He make Jerusalem a praise in the earth." It seems obvious that the Lord Jesus wants the redeemed to be involved in the enforcement of His triumph, and the execution of His will. Why does the Lord need remembrancers? Why should He need reminding of something that He has already revealed to be His purpose? Why does He command us to be involved in His burden and purpose for Zion; indeed to take no rest and give Him no rest until He fulfils it?

Here is an amazing mystery, and it is in the understanding of this mystery that finally we arrive at the heart of the matter. The Lord Jesus has absolute sovereign authority. There is no advance He cannot make; no purpose He cannot fulfil; no obstacle He cannot overcome; no problem He cannot solve; with Him nothing is impossible! However, He longs for the fellowship of those whom He has redeemed; He wants us to be freewill offerings, volunteers in the day of His army. Under His command, as His soldiers we are to see that His purpose is fulfilled.

We are to be his remembrancers, as secretaries to Him, and remind Him of His appointments which He must keep. We are to take His Word as it is applied by the Holy Spirit to the practical situations and problems which we are facing and stand on that Word until it is fulfilled. The incredible truth is that He invites us to be involved in the fulfilment of His purpose. He longs for us to be in such a real union with Himself, in such a living fellowship with Him, that together we will see His triumph registered in all kinds of practical situations, worldwide, national, and local.

His people who are freewill offerings, a volunteer army in the day of His army, are a peculiar treasure to Him, like jewels which radiate His light, His beauty, and His glory. They have entered His heart and remain exceedingly precious to Him. These treasured people who are freewill offerings, are like the woman, who before His death, broke her alabaster cruse of spikenard upon the Lord Jesus. She entered into His heart, as did none of the other disciples, and ministered to Him. Those who are freewill offerings to the Lord in the day of His power, of His army, have likewise identified

196

themselves with the Lord Jesus and ministered to Him. They will never be forgotten of Him.

OTHER BOOKS PRINTED BY CHRISTIAN TESTIMONY MINISTRY

Speakers: **Titles:**

Dana Congdon- Marriage, Singleness, and the Will of God
Recovery and Restoration
The Holy Spirit
Hebrews

AJ Flack- The Tent of His Splendour

Stephen Kaung- Acts
Be Ye Therefore Perfect
Called Out unto Christ
Called to the Fellowship of God's Son
(I Corinthians Series)
Divine Life and Order
For Me to Live is Christ
Glorious Liberty of the Children of God
God's Purpose for the Family
I Will Build My Church
Meditations on the Kingdom
Recovery
Spiritual Exercise
Spiritual Life (II Corinthians Series)
Teach Us to Pray
The Cross
The Fullness of Christ (Revelation)
The Headship of Christ
The Kingdom and the Church
The Kingdom of God
The Last Call to the Churches
The Life of Our Lord Jesus
The Life of the Church
The Lord's Table
Two Guideposts for Inheriting the Kingdom
Vision of Christ (Revelation)
Who Are We?
Why Do We So Gather?
Worship

Lance Lambert- Be Ye Ready
Called Unto His Eternal Glory
God's Eternal Purpose
In the Day of Thy Power

Jacob I Have Loved
Living Faith
Lessons from the Life of Moses
Love Divine
My House Shall Be a House of Prayer
Preparation for the Coming of the Lord
Reigning with Christ
Spiritual Character
Gospel of the Kingdom
The Importance of Covering
The Last Days and God's Priorities
The Prize
The Supremacy of Jesus Christ
Thine is The Power
Thou Art Mine
T. Austin Sparks- The Lord's Testimony and the World's Need
Harvey Cedar's Conference
Heavenly Vision
Spiritual Responsibility
Congdon, Hile, Kaung- Spiritual Ministry
Spiritual Authority
Spiritual House
Spiritual Submission
Stephen Kaung- Spirituality
Spiritual Knowledge
Spiritual Power
Spiritual Reality
Spiritual Value
Spiritual Blessing
Spiritual Discernment
Spiritual Warfare
Spiritual Ascendancy
Spiritual Mindedness
Spiritual Perfection
Spiritual Fullness
Spiritual Sonship
Spiritual Stewardship
Spiritual Travail
Spiritual Inheritance
Walk Worthy of the Kingdom of God
God's Testimony and Way
Christian Family Conference
Hile, Kaung, Lambert -The King is Coming

CPSIA information can be obtained at www.ICGtesting.com
Printed in the USA
LVOW100206050713

341511LV00008B/226/P